God's

Priceless

Woman

By

Wanda Kennedy Sanseri

God's Priceless Woman

© 1990 Wanda Kennedy Sanseri, revised 1991, revised 1997

Published by Back Home Industries
PO Box 22495; Milwaukie, OR 97269

Printed in the United States of America
ISBN 1-880045-04-4

DEDICATION

GOD'S PRICELESS WOMAN
is dedicated to my husband,
Gary
and our three sons,
Samuel
Daniel
Michael
who have enlarged my vision
and helped me complete this work.

This book is also dedicated to
the memory of my deceased husband,
Steve Kennedy
who led me to the Lord and
helped me in the early stages of this study.

Titus 2:3-5

A Woman's Personal Life: Prerequisite to Training Others

The older women likewise, that they be reverent in behavior (Lessons 1-6)
not slanderers (Lessons 7-8)
not given to much wine (Lessons 9-10)
teachers of good things (Lessons 11-12)

A Woman's Ministry to Others: Topics for Training Others

that they admonish the young women
to love their husbands (Lessons 13-14)
to love their children (Lessons 15-16)
to be discreet, chaste (Lessons 17-18)
homemakers (Lessons 19-20)
good (Lessons 21-22)
obedient to their own husbands (Lessons 23-24)

Results

that the Word of God be not blasphemed.

TABLE OF CONTENTS

Section/Title   **Page**

How to Get the Most Out of GPW vii
Introduction: A Proper Vision : The Secret to Success ix

A Woman's Personal Life : Prerequisite To Training Others

Lesson 1 : The Titus 2 Model 1
Lesson 2 : Proverbs 31: An Example of Titus 2 7

Lesson 3 : Hannah: A Woman Who Fears God 13
Lesson 4 : Fearing God 21

Lesson 5 : Mary: A Woman Who Reverences God 27
Lesson 6 : Reverencing God 33

Lesson 7 : Miriam: A Woman Who Speaks Unkindly 39
Lesson 8 : Speaking With Kindness 45

Lesson 9 : Queen Esther: A Woman Of Self-Control 53
Lesson 10 : Gaining Self-Control 59

A Woman's Ministry To Others : Topics For Training Others

Lesson 11 : Eve: A Woman Who Set A Bad Example 67
Lesson 12 : Training Younger Women By Example 73

Lesson 13 : Mary: a Woman Who Loved Her Husband 81
Lesson 14 : Encouraging Love For Husbands 87

Lesson 15 : Jochebed: A Woman Who Loved Children 95
Lesson 16 : Encouraging Love for Children 103

Lesson 17 : Sarah: A Woman Who Modeled Purity 111
Lesson 18 : Encouraging Purity 117

Lesson 19 : Priscilla: A Woman Who Worked at Home 125
Lesson 20 : Encouraging Homeworking 133

Lesson 21 : Dorcas: A Woman Who Did Good Deeds 141
Lesson 22 : Encouraging Good Deeds 149

Lesson 23 : Rebekah: A Woman Who Betrayed Her Husband 157
Lesson 24 : Encouraging Submission to Husbands 163

Lesson 25 : Ruth: A Single Priceless Woman 171
Lesson 26 : Proverbs 31: A Married Priceless Woman 177

Acknowledgements

I feel indebted for the support and encouragement of the believers at Fairhaven Bible Chapel in San Leandro, California where I fellowshipped for twelve years. I especially acknowledge Jean and June Gibson who guided me like parents both spiritually and practically and Ron and Lorene Chin who imparted to me their own souls. I owe appreciation to Lynette Goodell Keith who patiently discipled me as a new Christian and to my writer's support group led by Ethel Herr. I am glad Kathy Peak directed me to the group and helped me continue while I still lived in the San Francisco Bay Area. Larry Clark patiently directed the development of my writing skills and Cathy Duffy edited the study.

I appreciate the leaders of groups across the country that field-tested the material for me like Karen Thompson and Sharon Reinking. I am thankful for the insights and direction of Carol Stabler. At various stages of the work I had technical support from Dan Brown, Kathy Ormsby, Sheron Buttler, Pete Lertn, and many others too numerous to name. Sue Brown, Connie Conley and others watched my children to free me for valuable periods of unbroken writing time. Terry Buchanan edited the manuscript for me.

HOW TO GET THE MOST OUT OF *GPW*

The following guidelines will make the training of God's Priceless Woman more meaningful and more effective in your life.

1. BE A PART OF A GROUP. Although you can study this material privately, we recommend that you take the course with other women either on a one-on-one basis or a small group situation. Diversified groups (different ages and marital status) as well as special interest groups (i.e. young singles only, or home school moms) have used GPW with an equal measure of success.

2. ATTEND REGULARLY. The first week can be a get acquainted time followed by 26 sessions with homework lessons. Women should attend all sessions in order to obtain maximum benefit from the study. If possible, enroll in the beginning as the lessons are progressive and cumulative.

The schedule can vary. If time does not permit a full 26 or 27 weeks, the lessons can be combined two at a time and completed in 13 or 14 weeks. Busy women who find a weekly session difficult could consider meeting bi-monthly. One group spent a year studying together twice a month.

3. DO YOUR HOMEWORK. See the study guide questions in this book. Ideally these homework questions should be answered before reading the notes for the lesson. The notes help clarify and reinforce the concepts learned from original investigation of the Word. Remember to always use the Word as the primary source over any human commentary.

4. SELECT A PRAYER PARTNER. Establish one or more prayer partners from the group the first week of class. If possible spend time daily praying for each other and at least once a week praying together either in person or by phone.

5. KEEP A DIARY OF DEVOTIONS. We recommend a personal notebook for daily time with the Lord. Part of Lesson 6 will involve sharing applications from the private quiet times you have had that week.

6. SELECT A DOMESTIC SKILL PROJECT. Many groups enjoy adding work with domestic projects. Some have demonstrations each week. Other groups encourage individuals to select an area to be developing during the course. The final night ladies may bring their projects to class to share. Skills to polish can be selected in cooking, sewing, needle crafts, arts and crafts, home decorating, gardening, grooming or child care.

7. MEMORIZE KEY VERSES. Committing to memory verses from Proverbs 31 and Titus 2:3-5 will aid meditation. Prayer partners who elect to do so should listen to each other recite at a time best for them.

I stumbled onto a passage only a few verses long that put everything in perspective. God DID intend for someone to teach me how to be a godly woman. He did not want me groping, pursuing the meaningless call of the world. Titus 2:3-5 admonishes older women to teach the younger women. The challenge carries a warning. If older women do not train younger women then God's Word will be discredited.

How should I respond to my discovery? At twenty-three I could hardly be called an older woman. But young women some day become old. I wanted to prepare for that day.

Several years later we moved across the country. My burden moved me to action sooner than I expected. I observed the single high school, college and career girls in our new church, Fairhaven Bible Chapel. I remembered my own need for someone wiser. I was only a few years older, but I felt responsible to share the secrets I had learned. In the fall of 1974, with the approval of my church leaders, I invited sixteen girls to join me for a three month Bible study. This nucleus of girls in San Leandro, California inspired the first draft of God's Priceless Woman.

Recognizing my own inadequacies, and the need to involve older women in the lives of these girls, I set up a secret prayer pal system. Each student had one older Christian woman from the church who promised to pray daily for her during the three months of our study. I gave the older women a copy of the class outline and made suggested requests for each week. The last night of the series the older women hosted a banquet. Each girl shared what she had learned and met the woman who had especially prayed for her. Age barriers softened and both generations were blessed for the interchange.

Later my husband and I had the opportunity to train couples in our church for leadership responsibilities. I learned something that totally surprised me. It shouldn't have, perhaps, but it did. Singles and married people are not all that different. The wives needed the same foundational concepts I had studied with the younger girls. Applications may vary, but the principles remained constant. I adapted God's Priceless Woman for use in training these young wives and mothers.

Life is not static. In my early thirties I faced a new personal test. My husband and the father of our three pre-school age boys died of brain cancer. A tragedy? I can think of few things harder and yet God in his own way had prepared me. Principles I had uncovered in God's Priceless Woman worked to sustain me and give me purpose during the stress. My vision to train women helped me see this as a time of opportunity. As a married woman I had taught singles things I had wished some one had taught me when I was unmarried. Now as a single-again woman I could live out these ideals. I read that, as a single parent, the odds were against my ever remarrying. I understood a new challenge, the possibility of accepting permanent single life. My own healthy marriage had insulated me from understanding the hurts many experience, but when I lost my mate my ministry circle grew to other single-again women, divorcees, widows, and women with weak male leadership at home.

Groups as far away as Canada and Colorado heard about <u>God's Priceless Woman</u> and requested permission to use the Bible study. My attempt to meet a revision deadline led to a special surprise from the Lord. One lesson troubled me. I needed a fresh evaluation. On Saturday night I prayed for the Lord to send some one to help. On Sunday Gary Sanseri from Portland, Oregon spoke at our church. I could tell he had a deep walk with the Lord. Slow moving traffic after the service blocked the exit and just "happened" to stall me beside him. He introduced himself and raised the topic of the lesson I prayed about the night before. Since the lesson "just happened" to be tucked in my Bible, and since he had already studied the subject independently, I asked him to edit it for me. Gary kindly agreed as we parted ways. He left to return to his home 700 miles north.

I did not know how significant that brief encounter would be, not only for the development of the study, but for my own personal life. Gary mailed my lessons as he promised. His input was exactly what I needed, but he did not stop there. He enclosed a nine page personal letter. I had prayed for an editor. God gave me much more. A five minute "chance" encounter grew into a life-time partnership. A year later I married Gary. A new husband helped enlarge my ministry perspective.

In 1984 a Christian from the Los Angeles area, 1300 miles south, requested permission to use the course at Claremont Bible Chapel. The Bible study group in LA included young singles, newlyweds, mothers with small children, mothers with teenagers and ladies from the Christian retirement home. This group dynamically proved that universal principles are not restricted to age or station in life.

A vision born out of personal need took seed and grew. In 1990 we officially published <u>God's Priceless Woman</u>. What had circulated in Xeroxed copies across America can now be more easily purchased. In 1993 Christliche Literatur-Verbreitung published <u>Kostbarer als Korallen</u>, a German translation. Others have requested permission to translate the work as well. Whether we are young or old, single, married, or single again, live in North America, South America, Europe, Asia, or Africa, the same Scriptural admonitions stand. My prayer is that an army of women all over the world will grasp the vital calling God has given to Christian ladies to follow Him and to train others to do likewise.

A divorcee recently wrote me to express appreciation for this study. "Looking back I can't help wondering," she said, "that if someone mature in the Lord had loved enough to see a sister struggling and stepped in to teach her the way to be a godly woman, a divorce may have been prevented, and a marriage saved." She is now willing to reach out to help someone else. May we fill our ranks with older women equipped and available to mentor others. "The hoary head is a crown of glory, if it be found in the way of righteousness" (Proverbs 16:31). Let us start by training our daughters from their youth for this lifelong work.

---

1 Mary La Bouma, <u>The Creative Homemaker</u>, (Bethany Fellowship: Minneapolis, Minnesota,1973),p. 169. Used by permission.

A PROPER VISION: THE SECRET TO SUCCESS

1. The Bible warns that "where there is no vision the people perish" (Proverbs 29:18a). We as women need to know where we are going.   Evaluate your concept of womanhood. How do you feel about yourself?   Explain.

    How have your ideas changed since you became a Christian? (If you have been a Christian since you were young, how has your concept of womanhood changed over the years?)

2. Think of a contemporary woman you admire. Why do you esteem her? How has she motivated you?

3. Think of a contemporary woman who has been a negative influence on your life. Can you name some results of this negative influence?

4. Think of a woman from the Bible that you respect. What makes her outstanding in your eyes?

5. Read Titus 2:3-5. List the qualities mentioned. Identify the opposites of each.

Qualities Listed in Titus 2:3-5	Opposites

    Which qualities named in questions 1-4 are covered by the Titus description?

    Do any of the qualities you esteem conflict with the Titus description?

6. If possible select a prayer partner. See "How to Get the Most of GPW" point four.

A PROPER VISION : THE SECRET TO SUCCESS

My palms sweated as I clenched my hands and waited. The results would be announced soon. Did I win? I desired more than anything to be the first woman elected, for the world to see me as capable, important, in control, a woman who matters. These were the sixties, the early days of the feminist movement. Few women had broken into areas previously dominated by men. I did have one advantage. My father, a liberal minister, had groomed me for leadership. Since my fifteenth birthday, he had periodically turned his pulpit over to me for "Youth Sunday" or as a substitute for him after he suffered one of his kidney attacks. But would my peers accept me for this new honor in church leadership?

"A hundred churches are represented here today," began the presiding officer, "and I have the pleasure to announce to you that your newly elected District Youth President is..." I closed my eyes, trying hard to not care. The speaker paused for emphasis and then announced clearly, "Wanda Wise!"

I shrieked in delight and headed for the platform. Could it be true? Had I been chosen? I was one step closer to my dream, the chance to be the first woman bishop in my denomination. On the way to the front I spotted Mike, one of my opponents. He attempted a smile, but he could not disguise his hurt. His football player shoulders drooped in dejection, shame. My joy was his agony. He had not only lost; he had lost to a woman. The vision of Mike haunted me. Had my dream been wrong? I reviewed all my qualifications. I could do a good job. Was that the point? Was it a victory? Did I really get what I wanted? I tried to shake off my questions and enjoy my new honor.

I entered college as a religion major. My junior year a large church hired me as part-time youth director. I was the only woman applicant among a group of men applying for a job always before held by men. I had proved that I could gain predominance over men, but when I watched the effect on the men, my victory felt hollow. Did my dream promote my interest over the best interest of others? I wanted to glorify God with my life. How did he want to use me?

Then I did something I had never seriously done before. I started reading the Bible. My need to exalt myself and compete with men faded. I would soon realize how inadequately I had been prepared for womanhood.

I graduated from college with education credentials and started teaching high school English. Six months later I married Steve Kennedy. I planned to be the best wife possible in my spare time after school. But having a kitchen, even a sunny one, did not automatically make me a proficient cook. I had to refer to a cookbook for simple tasks, scrambling eggs, or cooking corn on the cob. I overspiced and undercooked many meals. Society had trained me for anything but my feminine role in marriage. I longed to be the perfect wife, but when? Every night I came home exhausted and loaded down with papers to grade or lesson plans to prepare for the next day. I felt trapped in combat with myself. Weary at night from teaching all day, I'd sometimes resent when my husband needed me. Other times I'd resent take-home work that interfered with my marriage relationship. If I wanted to or not, I didn't have time for Steve.

In place of my earlier desire to find a significant place out-side the home, I yearned to be a godly homemaker. Two years later my decision to quit teaching shocked everyone. I had achieved "success." Why should I give it up for the "drudgery and boredom" of the home? Mary LaGrand Bouma in her book <u>The Creative Homemaker</u> summarizes my discovery.

> If we choose not to do this very special job [homemaking],
> it will simply not get done;
> the mothering, the nurturing, the comforting and caring
> that fills the committed homemaker's day
> will simply be lost,
> and society will be impoverished.
> Children will not get the spiritual guidance they need.
> Lonely teenagers will not be listened to.
> Many people with problems will not be ministered to,
> many sick folk will go unvisited.
> A special human quality will disappear from our culture.
>
> Women can give up their jobs
> as clerks, engineers, sales people, doctors—
> other people will step in
> and the world will go on as smoothly as before.
> It will be business as usual.
> The groceries will still be sold,
> trucks loaded with merchandise will still roll across our highways,
> and Wall Street will carry on.
>
> Not so with homemaking.
> We are the special people into whose hands
> the country and the world have been entrusted.
> When we leave this job the world does not go on as before.
> It falters and begins to lose its way.
> We homemakers are indispensable. [1]

I realized that, as a woman, I faced enough challenge to keep me busy and fulfilled, but I felt cheated about one thing. Why had no one told me before? In my years of preparation, why had so much of my energy been poured into fruitless, frustrating endeavor?

STUDY GUIDE   LESSON 1

THE TITUS 2 MODEL

Read Titus 2: 1-5 in as many translations as possible. Answer the following questions.
(Your answers do not need to be exhaustive. Each of these points will be considered in
depth in separate lessons.)

1. All women are not ready to teach others. What prerequisites does Paul name?

   respectful in all they do
   not speaking evil of others
   not to be heavy drinkers
   teachers of goodness

2. How can a woman be reverent to God? Why do you think this quality is named first?

   ① *in her appearance, in her manner of speech*
   in all her actions
   ② *Your walk & your talk must agree*
   "What you do speaks so loud that the world can't hear what you say."

3. Why is tongue control so important for women? Can you think of an example when
   God's name has been dishonored or His work hindered by a slandering woman?

   much damage can be done by gossip - not God honoring
   Miriam - rose up against Moses
   Eve -

4. What does self-control mean? Why is it important for a godly woman to not be
   addicted to wine or <u>any excess</u>? Why is purity so crucial?

   ① *to be able to control your actions & desires*
   ② *a person is not in self-control if they drink too much*
   ③ *your body is a temple of God. Impurity can cause*
   much damage & can have lasting consequences

5. How can we inspire in another a love for husband, children and home? In your
   observation, what happens when a woman refuses to adapt to her husband?

   ① *by our example - respect for husband. speaking kindly*
   about them & not evil. pray for each other
   ② *there would be much discontent & trouble in*
   the home.

6. What could be considered good things to teach?

   to be charitable - helping others.
   spiritual guidance (pray)
   how a marriage is compared to Christ
   own time w/ God

A Power of a Praying wife - Stomie o'Marsh

THE TITUS 2 MODEL

Our vision of what is important effects our actions. Hilary Cosell's story in LADIES' HOME JOURNAL entitled, "Did We Have the Wrong Dreams?" illustrates how visualized aspirations can influence our lives.

A televised advertisement she saw as a pre-teen made a lasting impression. She explains:

> **The commercial was unforgettable.**
> **A montage of fashionable women flashing by in the cityscape—**
> **woman after woman,**
> **each looking more attractive,**
> **more important,**
> **more in control than the one before her.**
> **Smart tailored suits, attache cases, shapely pumps,**
> **heels clicking on the pavement, into skyscrapers,**
> **up stairs to rest behind big desks.**
> **All projecting an image that said**
> **confident, purposeful, serious...**
> **I kept the memory of those perfect businesswomen**
> **stored, buried for future use.**
> **A secret, silent motivator.**

Where did this vision get Hilary? She succeeded professionally with a career as a production assistant for network news. Was she happy?

"Imagine my shock, my near trauma," Hilary exclaims, "when I realized that I wanted something else. NEEDED something else. When I realized that I loved my job... and hated it. That it was my whole life. That it was no life at all."

"There I was, coming home from ten or twelve or sometimes more hours at work, pretty much shot after the day...Boring. Burned out. Good for nothing but to get up and do it all over again."

Hilary has a friend, Jane, a married woman with one son. Jane is a high-ranking editor with a national magazine. "I'm exhausted all the time," she confesses. "Much of my life seems to go by in a blur... I'm an overworked professional, an overtired mother, a fair-weather friend, and a part-time wife. Superwoman, huh?"

Value of Role Models

Like Hilary and Jane, I pondered the same questions. "Why did I feel so empty, so unfulfilled?" At a young age (my early twenties) I had everything I longed for—a successful career and a husband who loved me. I had listened carefully to the advice of the older women in my life. I acquired my college degree. I followed the woman's lib philosophy. The world's best left a void.

Then I met Pat. She had what I wanted. What was it? I watched her closely, looking for clues. A simple homemaker, she lacked the sophistication of my colleagues. Her husband seemed loving. He guided her, but not without respecting her views. Her home glowed with warmth. Being near her made me feel content and valuable.

By God's grace I had surrendered my life to Jesus months before, but attitudes take time to readjust. I asked Pat questions. She answered them with Scripture. Two passages transformed my thinking and gave me direction as a woman in life. Pat implanted in me a vision. She exposed my longing and showed me the answer to my need. My life could count. She demonstrated how.

The Scriptural mandate calls for more Pats, more women who understand the Creator's rich plan for women and who can model joy and fulfillment. Such a woman is described in Titus 2: 3-5. God uses three verses to overview where women are needed most, a message simple, yet profound.

> **Older women likewise are to be reverent in their behavior, not malicious gossips, nor enslaved to much wine, teaching what is good, that they may encourage the young women to love their husbands, to love their children, to be sensible, pure, workers at home, kind, being subject to their own husbands, that the word of God may not be dishonored (Titus 2:3-5).**

Hilary saw a commercial that influenced her life, but the dreams did not pass the test of time. Her goal did not satisfy. Titus 2:3-5, a vignette as short as a brief advertisement, became new, foundational, life verses for me. Titus 2 passage capsules God's message for women. I did not fully realize the implications, but I wanted to watch, observe and grow in understanding. In time I knew I would grasp the significance. It was a starting point, a foundation against which I could weigh life and other Scriptures.

Reasons to Develop the Qualities of Titus 2

There are at least three main reasons why every woman should seek to develop the qualities exemplified by the woman of Titus 2.

1. QUALITIES MODELED IN TITUS 2 ARE NEEDED REGARDLESS OF AGE OR MARITAL STATUS. The characteristics exemplified by the Titus passage are not restricted to wives or mothers. A spiritual understanding of life is required, but not a

wedding ring. The woman who helped me most in my role as a wife and mother is a childless woman who never married. She overcame her bitterness towards God and her jealousy of others who had families and she prayed for God to give her wisdom to minister to them. As a single woman she utilized the asset of availability and flexibility.

A woman's life is seasonal. Even women who do marry and nurture children have years with an empty nest. Many, like myself, unexpectedly lose their mate. Is ministry limited to any particular time in life? Not according to Titus.

2. EVERY WOMAN SHOULD ASPIRE TO TRAIN OTHERS. Paul exhorts godly women to guide others. Single women do not need to view preparation for marriage as a waste of time if they remain single. Even if a woman never marries she will have contact with other women who are wives and mothers and she is responsible before God to encourage them in their role.

Teenagers, older singles, newlyweds, women with small children, step-mothers, women with grown children, mother-in-laws, grandmothers, and widows, all have golden opportunities to learn things that will help others. A personal journal kept in prime learning times can be a valuable teaching tool some day.

Just as life does not begin with marriage, life should not be finished when the children leave home. Listen and observe throughout life. Apply wisdom on a day by day basis. Consider Titus 2: 3-5 from the Phillips paraphrase version:

> *...the old women should be examples of the good life,*
> *so that the younger women may learn to*
> *love their husbands and their children,*
> *to be sensible, and chaste,*
> *homelovers, kind-hearted*
> *and willing to adapt themselves to their husbands--*
> *a good advertisement for the Christian faith.*

Mary Pride in <u>All the Way Home</u> mirrors my experience. She claims:

> Every new Christian woman reads Titus 2:3-5 and goes on a search for an older woman who will train her.... I know, because a large number of them write to me complaining that **such a female is not to be found.** The older women are all busy with new careers or retirement plans. They have no time for their daughters' babies, or to give housecleaning lessons, or to hold a new couple's hands while they adjust to married life.....

> Most of us in this generation have to face the fact that we have to do two, or even three, generations' work at once unless we want our children stuck in a similar pickle.

I do hope that some of the older people in the church will realize they are needed and start sharing the Biblical parts of their experience and expertise. How wonderful it will be when the faithful older people finally realize that we need them, not to retire and make way for us, but to teach us!

But in the meantime, we have to help each other. We have to rediscover how to beget and raise our children according to the Bible; how to build up our family's spiritual, moral, intellectual and economic capital; and how to pass it on. [1]

3. NOBLE CHARACTER QUALITIES NEED TIME TO DEVELOP. Anything of true value takes time and effort. Step by step, little by little, each Christian woman can grow to more closely match the Lord's ideal.

God's evaluation of a woman of merit opposes the world's attitude in general. His ways are not our ways. Our society prepares women to compete with men, not to complete them. Our culture encourages mothers to "bravely" surrender our children to day-care centers and government schools.

"I'm always amazed," marvels Jo Berry, "that we are required to go to school and spend months, or even years learning to be secretaries, hairdressers, policewomen or doctors—but the way we learn to be wives and mothers is to get married and bear children." [2]

Untrained married women often feel insecure in the home and seek to find fulfillment in outside careers. The escape would not be necessary if a woman saw the potential in a home ministry. Women who spend their best years in the outside work force, delegating their home responsibilities to others, have less to teach younger women later in life. They retire from their outside job to an unnecessary void.

In the following lessons we will analyze Titus 2 bit by bit. Character studies of women from the Old and New Testaments will help illustrate the various qualities listed. Modern day examples are also included to increase understanding of principles discussed.

---

1 Mary Pride. <u>All the Way Home.</u> (Crossway Books: Westchester, Illinois, 1989), pp. 89-90.

2 Jo Berry. <u>The Happy Home Handbook.</u> (Fleming H. Revell Co.: Old Tappan, NJ, 1976), p. 16. Used by permission.

PROVERBS 31: AN EXAMPLE OF TITUS 2

1. Read Proverbs 31:10 in as many translations as possible. The word describing this woman in the original Hebrew is "chayil." List various ways the word has been translated into English. ~worthy   noble in character

strength of character
women of strength - Strong in wisdom + grace though a weaker vessel
women of resolution - strong in principles

2. Find Titus 2 qualities illustrated in Proverbs 31: 10-31.

reverence for God *vs. 30*   love for children *vs 13, 21, 27*

tongue control, *26*   home lover *vs. 13-15, 27*

self-control *vs 12, 27*   pure *vs 30, 29*

love for husband *vs. 11, 27*   teacher of good *vs 26, 20*

3. What does Scripture say about the ease of finding a woman of God's standard (Proverbs 31:10; Ecclesiastes 7:28)?

they are rare,
more precious than jewels

To what is she compared? What can we learn from this analogy?

real jewels - precious jewels.
the God must build the inner character

4. In your opinion, why would the description of an ideal wife and mother be given as a guideline for a single man searching for a mate (Proverbs 31)? How can a single person model these qualities?

Prov 2:19

① to know what to look for in a woman. It is not outward beauty, but her life style + godly qualities
② How they occupy their time; especially "free" time, - helping others, their talk. ③ How they will adapt to wife + mother.

5. King Lemuel's queen mother wisely counseled her grown son. (Proverbs 31:10-31). Using her as an example, explain the importance of older godly women. Describe a quality you have seen in another woman's life that you have imitated in your life. *they are needed to instruct + help younger women.*
- helping the poor, - devoted to knowing scripture

6. The virtuous woman's dominant characteristic is the "fear of the Lord" (Proverbs 31:30). Tell briefly how you became a Christian (if you have) and share some of the benefits you have experienced since conversion.

the joy of prayer Rom 8:28

PROVERBS 31: AN EXAMPLE OF TITUS 2

"Her worth is far above rubies"
(Prov. 31:10, NKJV)

Sharon, my friend the beauty queen, was lovely to behold. Her green eyes sparkled like emeralds and she floated gracefully when she walked. Charming, captivating, seemingly desirable. Her husband committed suicide.

Polly, my friend the business woman, won recognition as an outstanding achiever. Polished, smooth, and articulate. Her husband divorced her for another woman.

Sue, an attractive acquaintance known for friendliness and fun, developed the gift of flattery. Others felt drawn to her. People called her an ideal mother. One day without warning she deserted her husband and children for another man.

I considered the women in my life, ones who cared for me directly and ones I observed. Many were like Solomon's wives. He moaned, "I find more bitter than death the woman who is a snare, whose heart is a trap and whose hands are chains. The man who pleases God escapes from her" (Ecclesiastes 7:26). Occasionally there is a bright spot, a woman who stands out as special. I can name some, but they are rare.

What is the perfect woman? Solomon had his pick of women, but used the wrong standards. Perhaps he looked for the beauty queen type—lovely, intelligent, and talented. But the most gorgeous women often feel insecure because the praise they thrive on is dependent on externals. Maybe he felt attracted to the manipulative charmer. He should have listened to King Lemuel's queen mother's advice.

Beauty queens can be godly women and some wonderful women have been deserted by undiscerning men. (Even Jesus Christ faced rejection). But in Proverbs we are given an ideal model. Her husband rose up and praised her. Why?

God's model woman may or may not be beautiful, talented or rich. Her value rests not on innate qualities, but on developed godly character. Such a woman is graphically described in Proverbs 31:10-31. Any woman can pattern after her. Few ever do.

Compared to a Precious Jewel

In Proverbs 31:10 the adjective describing this woman has been translated "virtuous" (KJV), "excellent" (NASB), "noble in character" (NIV), and "good" (RSV). The Hebrew word "chayil" when used elsewhere in Scripture is most commonly translated "worthy" or "army." Thus an ideal woman is worth an entire army to her family and her nation. She is priceless.

Compared to the precious gem, the ruby, this woman is valuable and extremely hard to find. In fact the godly woman is so exceptional that King Solomon, who knew at least 1,000 women personally (he had 700 wives and 300 concubines), exclaimed, "a man among a thousand have I found, but a woman among all these I have not found" (Ecclesiastes 7:28).

The ruby, in a large size, is one of the costliest jewels. A certified gemologist explained the value of the ruby. Currently, a natural one carat ruby sells in excess of $1500. "The trick," the gemologist said," is to find one. They are increasingly rare." The synthetic replica, however, will sell for $15. Like a ruby, a woman can take on the outer appearance of a godly woman, but unless God is forming her inner character, the resulting woman will be a counterfeit. In our own strength we can at best become a dimestore trinket. Our goal should be to let the Lord mold us into the real gem.

Valued as a Model for all Women

Many people reading Proverbs 31 see only the profile of a married woman with children. Single people often disregard her example as irrelevant. Yet Scripture is not so restrictive. King Lemuel's queen mother described the ideal woman to her bachelor son (Proverbs 31:1). Why did she give the profile of a perfect wife and mother to her single son when more than likely he would marry a virgin?

Ask a typical group of teenagers what they desire in a future mate and the majority will give short-sighted qualities: hair color, figure, ability to dance or be a good date. King Lemuel's mother knew that the qualities that impress a young man—beauty, charm and popularity—are not the characteristics needed to sustain a lasting marriage.

She wanted her son to evaluate a future mate in terms of enduring qualities. Somehow he should visualize a single woman's ability to adapt to the role of wife and mother by observing her response to life as a single woman.

Some older women hesitate to study Proverbs 31. They feel it is too late for them. The Lord never intended for the older women to sit and aimlessly watch others. King Lemuel's mother had probably passed her own prime. Perhaps her children had left home. But her ministry did not stop when her son became King. The younger generation needs the example and guidance of those more mature. When the older women drop the ball God's honor is jeopardized (Titus 2:3-5).

Remembered for Spiritual Qualities

The first requirement for God's priceless woman is not externals, like beauty or charm, but rather the "fear of the Lord" (Proverbs 31:30). Knowing that she fears the Lord tells us she is ever aware that God is watching and weighing every one of her thoughts, attitudes, words and actions. Albert E. Horton explains, "Fearing God means simply giving to Him the place which is rightfully His as His creatures." [1]

The godly woman differs from the talented, but unsaved, woman in her basic motivation for achievement. Unlike the woman who seeks self-glory, God's priceless woman's main goal in life is to bring glory to the Lord Jesus Christ. Realizing that God holds the secrets of the universe, she searches the Bible like one hunting silver and hidden treasures. She gains true wisdom (Proverbs 2:1-6). She can be compared to the godly woman in Titus 2, reverent, and self-controlled in actions and speech.

<u>Identified with Support Ministries</u>

The family is her main priority. Other jobs are extensions of her home, not conflicting interests. She sells home-sewn products which she makes in her spare time and uses the proceeds to buy a personal vineyard. She redeems the time, but does not neglect her husband or children in the name of self-advancement. Her home becomes a center of outreach (Proverbs 31:20), but not at the expense of her family which is her higher responsibility. Like the Titus 2 model she can be called a home lover, concerned for the needs of her husband and children.

This contented woman considers the role of homemaker challenging and exciting. She is too creative and industrious to be bored. A gourmet cook (31:22), a gardener (31:16), and a seamstress (31:22), she also is talented in needlecrafts like weaving (31:13) and tapestry (31:22). "She perceiveth that her merchandise is good" (31:18) and, therefore, works "willingly with her hands" (31:13), or according to the NIV version, "works with eager hands." Her family does not feel that they are a burden to her. Instead they sense her joy in providing for both their immediate and long-range needs. Not only does she rejoice in the quality of her own labor, but she also receives the blessing of freeing her mate to succeed in the community.

Although this talented, industrious woman has the qualities necessary for success in any career outside the home, she understands the unique contribution of a dedicated homemaker. The benefits of her life extend past her home to influence the community. Like the Titus 2 model, she dresses modestly and reaches out doing good—helping the physically poor and the spiritually needy (Proverbs 31:20).

<u>Rewarded for Others-Centered Life</u>

The rewards for the virtuous woman are manifold.

1. SATISFACTION FROM HER HANDIWORK. She finds fulfillment from the creative touches she has added to the world around her: an attractive meal, an artistically arranged living room, a well-planned wardrobe, or personal gifts for others.

2. PRAISE FROM HER CHILDREN. Her family praises her for the personal work

she has unselfishly done for them. Adult children, who can reflect on the value of her training, rise up to commend her (Proverbs 31:28). The oldest brother of Charles Spurgeon praised his mother as "the starting point of all greatness and goodness that any of us by the grace of God enjoyed." [2] This nineteenth century woman delivered seventeen children, nine of whom died in infancy. Her second-born became one of the greatest ministers of all time, affectionately known as "the prince of preachers."

3. PRAISE FROM HER HUSBAND. Many men who have helped reshape the world held high esteem for their wives.

Martin Luther, a forty-one year old ex-monk, married Katherine von Bora, an escaped nun sixteen years his junior. Both needed each other and a marriage of convenience grew into a deep love relationship. Luther, though a master theologian, "was totally incapable of organizing the affairs of even the smallest households."[3] Katie freed him to expand his ministry. As a single man, Luther viewed marriage as a necessity for the flesh, but after wedlock he saw it as an opportunity for the spirit. Luther called Galatians, the epistle which led to his conversion and, therefore, the book closest to his heart, "my Katharine von Bora." [4] He claimed, "To have peace and love in marriage is a gift which is next to the knowledge of the Gospel."[5]

John Calvin, another key leader in the Protestant Reformation, described his wife, Idelette, as "the best companion of my life." He extolled her saying, "She has been a faithful aid in all my ministry. Never has she hindered me in the slightest." [6]

4. RESPECT FROM GODLY LEADERSHIP OF THE COMMUNITY. A godly woman will have a good reputation among the spiritual leaders and they will praise her to her husband when he "sits at the gates" with the other men (Proverbs 31:31).

5. APPROVAL IN HEAVEN. Her rewards are not limited to this life. God will also honor her in eternity (the gates of heaven) when her spiritual "works" are tried by fire (1 Corinthians 3:11-15). In that day it will be confirmed that this "ruby" is indeed a precious jewel.

---

1 Horton, Albert E.. "Aspects of Fear," Interest Magazine. September, 1978, p.5. Used by permission.

2 Bacon, Ernest W.. Spurgeon: Heir of the Puritans. Arlington Heights, IL: Christian Liberty Press, 1996, p.2.

3 Petersen, William. Martin Luther Had a Wife. Wheaton, IL: Tyndale House, 1983, p. 15.

4 Ibid. p. 35.

5 Ibid. p. 34.

6 Beza, Theodore. The Life of John Calvin. Milwaukie, OR: Back Home Industries, 1996, p. 130.

HANNAH: A WOMAN WHO FEARS GOD

1. Read 1 Samuel 1:2-8. Describe Hannah's conflict. Who was responsible for Hannah's condition (v. 5)? *Hannah did not have a child & Penunnah did. She very much desired to have a child. the Lord had closed her womb.*

   How does God use challenges to bring blessing into our lives? *When we cannot solve the problem & we surrender it all to God, then God - if it is in His will - supply us with what we needed. We then realize it was all from Him.*

2. How did Hannah respond to her condition at first (v. 6-7)? Can you think of a conflict in your own life that affected you in a similar way? Explain. *she cried & could not eat.*

   What did she finally do to overcome her bitterness (v. 9-19)? *she prayed to God & vowed to give her child to God for His service "Cast all your cares upon Him for He careth for you."*

3. What principles can we learn from Hannah's prayer (1 Samuel 1:11)? *① our children are a gift from God. We are to dedicate them to God ② God hears and answers prayer. ③ God is concerned for the oppressed & afflicted*

4. Describe the changes in Hannah's attitude toward the Lord, and toward her husband (1 Samuel 1:19-2:1). *She returned home well & happy because 1. she honestly prayed to God 2. she received encouragement from Eli 3. she resolved to leave the problem w/ God.*

5. List some of the benefits that Hannah experienced as a result of her victory in dealing with her problem of barrenness (1 Samuel 1:27-28; 2:20-21; 3:19-21). *① she had a child. not only Samuel but 5 other children ② Samuel served the Lord in the Tabernacle*

   In light of 1 Samuel 1:27, how do you think Hannah would have reacted if she still did not conceive? Explain. *She fully realized that Samuel was from the Lord. She would have surrendered her barreness to God, because she gave Samuel back to God for His service*

6. Select one of the following verses. Apply the verse to Hannah's life and to your own life. (Proverbs 9:10; Proverbs 15:33; Proverbs 22:4; or Revelation 14:7). *When we humble ourself before God & fear Him - surrender our whole life to Him, it is the beginning of Wisdom, riches & eternal Life*

(Personal Question. Group sharing optional). Hannah voluntarily surrendered her most valuable possession to the Lord. Do you have something which you need to commit to Him today? If so write a prayer of commitment, yielding to the Lord your own life and the possessions or people you hold dear.

HANNAH: A WOMAN WHO FEARS GOD

". . . woman who fears the Lord , she shall be praised"
(Proverbs 31:30, NKJV).

The first wife taunted the new mate. She used her children as a wedge to earn the man's attentions. She had something only she could give. Living weapons. He tried to reassure his second wife. "Am I not better to you than ten sons?" But she would not listen. She felt second rate, second class, inadequate. If only she could have a child too. She fretted and went without food. Years passed. Time intensified the hurt. Then one day her focus shifted and Hannah found deliverance from depression. Her countenance lifted. She responded warmly to her husband and she received the desire of her heart. What caused the change?

Hannah spent years unsuccessfully wrestling with God in an area beyond her control. Then one day her motives shifted. Gone was the desire for vindication. Her eyes lifted from her own plight to focus on a higher purpose. She learned the first quality in Titus 2, the supreme quality in Proverbs 31. She learned to reverence or fear God.

Hannah Yielded Her Soul for Salvation

The most essential step to inner peace is yielding our souls to the Lord. We were created to bring honor to the Creator, not to ourselves. The Lord describes us as "created for my glory" (Isaiah 43:7). Our only eternal hope is to confess our sins, repent and accept the Lord's sacrifice. "He [Jesus] was wounded for our transgressions; he was bruised for our iniquities; the chastisement of our peace was upon him; and with his stripes we are healed" (Isaiah 53:5).

Hannah accepted the "Lord God Almighty" (1 Samuel 1:11) who would one day pay for her sins by His death and resurrection. She recognized that, "by strength no man shall prevail. The adversaries of the Lord shall be broken to pieces; From heaven He will thunder against them. The Lord will judge the ends of the earth" (1 Samuel 2: 9-10, NKJV). "Fear God and give glory to Him...and worship Him who made heaven and earth, the sea and springs of water" (Revelations 14:7 NKJV). To fear God is to surrender every aspect of our lives to His control.

Hannah Relinquished Her Personal Rights to God

We understand Hannah's desire for children. For a Jewish woman, barrenness was a cultural shame, a reason to suspect unconfessed sin. To make matters worse her husband Elkanah's other wife (Peninnah) mothered sons and daughters and taunted Hannah. "Her adversary also provoked her sore, for to make her fret, because the Lord had shut up her womb" (1 Samuel 1:6). Hannah became so absorbed in self-pity, she withdrew from everyday activities. The competition of another wife and the grief of empty arms overwhelmed her. "She wept and did not eat" (v.7).

Hannah's misery continued for years. Her bitterness darkened her human relationships and hindered her fellowship with the Lord. Her husband felt inadequate for her and he pleaded, "Hannah, why are you weeping? Why don't you eat? Why are you downhearted?" (v.8). Her worship was impaired. As long as Hannah focused on her desire for motherhood, she had no victory. God had a purpose for her life and His goal could not be fulfilled until Hannah accepted His divine control over the very thing she was helpless to change.

Blessings can come out of our sorrow, but not as long as we nurture bitterness. Hannah learned the secret to fruitfulness. She broke before God and confessed her frustration, anguish and grief. She poured out her heart. "She was in bitterness of soul, and prayed unto the Lord, and wept sore" (v.10). She went to Him to appeal for help.

When Hannah finally prayed in 1 Samuel 1:11 her attitude changed in several significant ways.

1. SHE HUMBLED HERSELF BEFORE GOD. Hannah prayed recognizing that she, a simple handmaid or maid-servant, was requesting a favor from the "Lord of hosts". She contrasted her unworthiness with His glory and strength. She acknowledged God's ability to change her barren state.

2. SHE FOCUSED ON THE GIVER AND NOT THE GIFT. Although God desires to bestow many blessings on His children, His love restrains Him from granting some requests. Often our wishes, though not bad in themselves, would not be for our best interests. Whenever a natural desire becomes an obsession to the point of idolization, God may lovingly protect us by withholding that wish (James 4:2). It was not until Hannah's focus returned to its rightful place that God felt free to fulfill her longing.

3. SHE RECOGNIZED CHILDREN AS A BLESSING, NOT A RIGHT. She did not pray, "You should give me a child because I deserve one." Hannah prayed "if thou wilt . . . remember me. . ." Children are a gift from God (Psalm 127:3).

4. SHE SAW BEYOND THE IMMEDIATE TO ETERNAL ISSUES. Her focus shifted from a desire for personal justification before Peninnah, to the need for a godly leader in Israel. When we crave the removal of a problem for personal advantage, frustration is inevitable. Instead of concentrating on the imperative urgency of the moment, like a child demanding candy, she adjusted her long range focus, accepting His sovereign wisdom and love. A yieldedness to God's plan freed her to worship Him.

5. SHE CONSIDERED THE NEEDS OF OTHERS. Israel needed a godly leader more than Hannah needed a child to enjoy. Hannah's desire for a son was no longer limited to personal need. Her request showed how she envisaged the need for leadership in the nation. She dedicated her son to be a Nazarite (Numbers 6:1-21), one set apart for special service to God, so that he could be raised up to offer spiritual light in

darkened times. The visible sign of a Nazarite man was long hair. Hence, Hannah promised "no razor will ever be used on his head" (v.11).

6. SHE PREFERRED GOD'S WILL BEING ACCOMPLISHED TO HAVING HER OWN WAY. Hannah demonstrated her heart change by offering to give up the very child she had longed so many years to receive. The request did not represent a bargain with God, but rather a true heart change.

Before she knew she had conceived, her sorrowful spirit changed. "So the woman went her way, and did eat, and her countenance was no more sad. And they rose in the morning early, and worshipped before the Lord" (1 Samuel 1:18-19). Relationships were restored with others not because she had the baby, but because she accepted her personal problem as something planned by God for a divine purpose. When Hannah gave birth to a child, she rejoiced in being able to give him back to God (1 Samuel 1:27-2:1).

Hannah Committed Her Future Dreams to the Lord

Hannah accepted the Lord as her personal Savior and she gained peace over a major area of frustration, her childless state. But Hannah also went a step deeper in her commitment to God. After Samuel's birth she voluntarily yielded her right to care for him and willingly committed to God her dreams for the future.

The sincerity of Hannah's prayer was tested over many years. In victory she not only yielded her right to her only son, but she did so joyfully (1 Samuel 1:27-2:1). She could have claimed excuses to withhold him. The sons of Eli were corrupt, "they knew not the Lord" (1 Samuel 2:17). But she left her son to live in the temple. "Samuel ministered before the Lord, being a child, girded with a linen ephod" (2:18). Annually Hannah made him a little coat. Each time she saw Samuel, she faced the temptation to reclaim him for her own, but each year she returned home alone. She was faithful to her voluntary commitment to give him to the Lord.

God honored Hannah's commitment over and above her greatest dreams. She learned that God's plans are for good. "Or what man is there of you, whom if his son ask bread, will he give him a stone? Or if he ask a fish, will he give him a serpent? If ye then, being evil, know how to give good gifts unto your children, how much more shall your Father which is in heaven give good things to them that ask him?" (Matthew 7:9-11)..."And everyone that hath forsaken houses, or brethren, or sisters, or father, or mother, or wife, or children, or lands, for my name's sake, shall receive an hundred fold and shall inherit everlasting life" (Matthew 19:29).

God Honored Hannah's Faith

Hannah's example demonstrates that the waiting seasons are often needed in order to have the full blessing to follow. She received a number of long-term benefits for her sacrificial commitment. Some of the blessings that came out of her struggle and victory were not evident in her lifetime. The full impact of her life will not be revealed until glory. But we will consider some of the rewards of her faith, realizing we only see the tip of the iceberg.

1. SHE INSPIRED WORSHIP IN OTHERS. Eli was spiritually dim. We find him sitting at the doorpost of the temple (1 Samuel 1:9), where priests were ordered to stand (Deuteronomy 10:8). Yet Hannah's sacrificial response to answered prayer inspired him to worship (1:28).

2. SHE HAD SOMETHING TO GIVE BACK TO GOD. Hannah had a priceless gift (1 Samuel 1:28). No sacrifices could please Him more than the gift of an only son (Luke 2:23).

3. SHE MODELED AN EFFECTIVE PRAYER LIFE. Not only is Hannah remembered for her model prayer (1 Samuel 1:10), but she also inspired others to pray (2:20), and her son Samuel became known as a man of prayer. As an adult he said, "God forbid that I should sin against the Lord in ceasing to pray for you; but I will teach you the good and the right way" (1 Samuel 12:12).

4. SHE GAINED A DEEPER APPRECIATION FOR THE CHARACTER OF GOD. After Samuel's dedication at the temple, Hannah praised God for His justice and fairness. As if in response to Peninnah's provocation about her barrenness, she exclaimed, "Talk no more so exceeding proudly... for the Lord is a God of knowledge, and by Him actions are weighed... so that barren has born seven; and she that hath many children waxed feeble" (1 Samuel 2:3-5).

5. SHE RECEIVED UNEXPECTED BONUSES. Hannah requested a son. God gave her the son she desired plus three additional sons and two daughters (1 Samuel 2:21). God answers over and above what we ask or even think (Ephesians 3:20).

6. HER FIRST BORN RECEIVED SPECIAL FAVOR. "And I will raise me up a faithful priest, that shall do according to that which is in mine heart and in my mind: and I will build him a sure house; and he shall walk before mine anointed forever" (1 Samuel 2:35). "And Samuel grew, and the Lord was with him, and did let none of his words fall to the ground" (3:19).

7. SHE HAD AN EFFECT ON NATIONS. During a period of spiritual corruptness, Hannah bore a godly son who was to become a major prophet and one of Israel's greatest judges (1 Samuel 3:19-21). Unlike his predecessors who did not even know God (2:12), this priest is remembered as a man of faith (Hebrews 11:1,2,32). Under the priestly rule of Eli and his immoral sons, the word of the Lord had been rare (1 Samuel 3:1), but because of Samuel, the Lord appeared again in Shiloh (3:21). Under his leadership the Israelites reclaimed the ark of the Lord which the Philistines had taken for spoil. The people turned from idols to serve the living God. Israel regained cities

lost in battle and made peace with the Philistines, a peace that extended throughout the lifetime of Samuel.

8. SHE INSPIRED COUNTLESS INDIVIDUALS FOR GENERATIONS TO COME. Because Hannah's story is recorded in the Bible, for centuries it has had an impact on others. Among those inspired by her commitment to God was Mary, the mother of Jesus. Luke 1:46-55 records Mary's prayer of praise which is almost a point by point paraphrase of Hannah's prayer found in 1 Samuel 2:1-10.

FEARING GOD

1. Define "fearing the Lord". The following verses might help. Psalm 31:19, Psalm 111:10, Psalm 112:1, Psalm 147:11, and Proverbs 8:13.

2. (Question for personal use--group sharing optional). What life situations of an uncontrollable nature have you battled with recently?

  - race or nationality
  - physical characteristic(s)
  - relatives or in-laws
  - mate (or lack of one)
  - death of someone you love
  - spiritual gift
  - health

  - age
  - sex
  - children (or lack of them)
  - lack of talents
  - station in life
  - finances
  - other (specify) _____

3. How did Job, the righteous man who suffered innocently, respond to his trials? (Job 23:1-12). What result came out of his suffering (Job 42:12)?

4. Sometimes suffering is used to deal with God's children who are not following Him or fearing Him. Why does he allow trial in the case of disobedient believers (Jeremiah 24:5-7; 29:11-14; 31:10-14)?

5. Select one of the following situations and explain how it can result in God's glory, our benefit and the benefit of others. You may choose additional verses to strengthen your point.

  - grief (2 Corinthians 1:3-4)
  - trials of many kinds (James 1:2-4)
  - troubles (2 Corinthians 4:16-18)
  - illness (2 Corinthians 12:7-10)
  - persecutions (1 Peter 4:12-14)

6. Can you cite an example from your own life where as an offshoot of a personal difficulty either you or an acquaintance of yours was able to bring special glory to the Lord? Explain.

FEARING GOD

"The Lord takes pleasure in those who fear Him,
in those who hope in His mercy"
(Psalm 147:11, NKJV).

I loosened my grip on the bed pillow I had been clinging to for comfort so I could untangle my feet from the mass of quilts knotted on my bed. As I struggled to free myself from the bed linen, I glanced into the mirror.

Droopy brown eyes stared back. People often admired my bright, big eyes. This morning they were puffy and swollen from a night of crying. The splotches of red on my face reminded me of the boy in fifth grade with me who had a large red birthmark on his cheek.

I had gone through nights like this before, more often than I wanted to remember. Tonight I had watched Dad, the victim of a terminal illness, carted off in a stretcher, tubes dangling from his body, blood staining his face. More frequently the drama centered around his funeral service. The sky would be overcast and grey. I would ride in the family car following the hearse containing Dad's body or sit in the front row of the church studying the casket and sobbing too hard to hear the memorial message. The setting varied but the story plot remained constant. In the imaginary world of my dreams, Dad died and I could not cope with the stress of his death.

The nightmares continued for years. Little did I know my Dad would live thirty more years before he died at age seventy. The fear of evil, a foreboding, helpless, tormenting emotion, can destroy, weaken and paralyze. My childhood fear of losing my father caused unnecessary anxiety and agony.

The year I turned twenty-three I found deliverance from morbid apprehension of impending danger. I discovered a new type of fear, a fear that produces positive results—cleansing and purifying me within and giving me peace and assurance regarding the future. I discovered the fear of the Lord.

The Fear That Leads to Salvation

"The fear of Lord is the beginning of knowledge, but fools despise wisdom and discipline" (Proverbs 1:7). Looking back, I recognize several steps that, by God's grace, led to my deliverance.

1. I REDIRECTED MY FEAR. Unknowingly I had feared Satan and the harm he could produce in my life. Matthew warns, "Do not be afraid of those who kill the body

but cannot kill the soul. Rather, be afraid of the one who can destroy both soul and body in hell" (Matthew 10:28). Satan has great power, but his effectiveness is limited by God, the supreme power. "' I am a great king,' says the Lord Almighty, 'and my name is to be feared among the nations'"(Malachi 1:14). God is a God of purity and justice. He is all powerful and all knowing. Before Him sinners should tremble. Every sin must be dealt with and He knows every wrong, including secret private thoughts. "It is a dreadful thing to fall into the hands of the living God" (Hebrews 10:31).

2. I REPENTED OF MY SINFULNESS BEFORE A HOLY GOD. I had felt cocky and certain about my eternal destiny, mentally rehearsing all the good things I had done to please God. But I never experienced peace until I confessed my sin and recognized my need to change (Isaiah 57:20-21). I could find others who had done worse than I had, but God does not grade on the curve. He sees motives and not just actions. My "goodness" to him was filthy rags (Isaiah 64:6). I deceived myself when I thought I met his standard (Romans 4:4). I needed a new heart which only He could give me.

3. I RECOGNIZED GOD AS A GOD OF BOTH JUSTICE AND LOVE. I deserved eternal judgement. "The soul that sinneth, it shall die" (Ezekiel 18:4). I called out for mercy, not based on my performance. I appealed to the work of Jesus Christ who sacrificially provided a way to escape the wrath I deserved. Only through His death and resurrection could I hope for victory over the grave. He bore my punishment so he could give me abundant life. In Him I found peace (Romans 5:1).

4. I MADE MY FIRST PRIORITY SERVING HIM (Matthew 6: 33-34). He not only cares about my eternal soul, but he also cares about my daily needs such as food, clothes, and even parental love. When I realized I could trust the LORD, with His foreknowledge, to help meet my real needs, the foreboding fears of "what if" ceased.

The Fear of the Lord for the Believer

The believer enters a personal relationship with God, a relationship that brings privilege, but can involve discipline (Hebrews 12:6-7). Misguided priorities or unconfessed sin can lead to material loss (Haggai 1:5), sickness or death (Acts 5: 1-ll; 1 Corinthians 11: 27-30), or loss of eternal rewards (1 Corinthians 3: 11-15). "Do not be deceived; God is not mocked: for whatsoever a man soweth, that shall he also reap"(Galatians 6:7).

Psalms and Proverbs abound with promises for the faithful, the one who fears God. "Blessed is every one who feareth the Lord, that walketh in his ways" (Psalm 128:1). "The Lord favors those who fear Him, those who wait for His lovingkindness" (Psalm 147:11, NASB).

Sometimes the innocent suffer temporarily, but an understanding of the nature of God can help the believer endure. Habakkuk's nation faced impending judgment and financial ruin. "Yet I will rejoice in the LORD," the prophet sang. "I will joy in the God of my salvation" (Habakkuk 3:18). Joy comes as a by-product of confidence in God, not from certainty in unpredictable circumstances.

God's sovereign love ultimately protects the faithful from wicked schemes, but sometimes, when it serves His end, He allows evil men to temporarily triumph (Psalm 37). Jacob suffered as an employee to a dishonest boss, his uncle. In time God observed the injustice and intervened (Genesis 31:6-13). Joseph's brothers sold him into slavery. Years later Joseph reassured them, "You intended to harm me, but God intended it for good to accomplish what is now being done, the saving of many lives" (Genesis 50:20).

Someday God will erase the pain of sin and death, but meanwhile believers, like others, struggle with the consequences of the fall. In our abnormal world God may display his love in helping us accept handicaps and limitations. He gives purpose to suffering.

God was in control when the boy in the New Testament was born blind "so the works of God could be made manifest in him" (John 9:3). Jesus had power over the fatal sickness of Lazarus, a sickness allowed "for the glory of God that the Son of God might be glorified thereby" (John 11:4). Paul received a thorn in the flesh to prevent self-pride and to manifest God's power.

God was in control when my thirty-five year old husband died of brain cancer. He upheld me and my fatherless children and in due time provided another godly husband for me and father for my three sons. The way God even turns the despair of life into something special is summarized well in Psalm 84: 5-7. Gary and I claimed these words as theme verses in our new life together. Whatever life held, our God would strengthen us to endure until He wipes away all our tears in heaven. See below the paraphrase written and sung for our wedding by our friend, Dave Crotzer .

"Happy are those who are strong in the Lord
Who follow in His steps.
When they walk though the Valley of Weeping
It becomes a place of springs
Where refreshing pools of blessing may gather after rains.
And they will go from strength to strength
Until they meet the Lord."

<u>Fearing God Leads to Total Commitment</u>

Freedom comes when we learn to trust Him. Our hearts hold dear many things. Some key examples include friends, marriage, children and a home. These things are good, but they are not "rights." **The Lord Himself is the only person that a Christian can have the assurance of never losing in this life.** Possessions can be destroyed, relationships can be severed by death, and children are designed to grow up and leave home.

When Job first learned of the series of trials facing him in one day (four separate tragedies which wiped out his material wealth and precipitated the sudden death of all ten of his children), he responded in a supernatural way. Job "shaved his head" (which showed he felt the grief intensely) and "fell down upon the ground and worshipped" (which showed he still trusted God as powerful and loving). Job said, "Naked came I from my mother's womb, and naked I shall return thither: The LORD gave and the LORD hath taken away: blessed be the name of the LORD." The text continues, "In all this, Job sinned not, nor charged God foolishly" (Job 1:20-22).

Job had a victory over this tremendous test because he did not believe God owed him anything. He saw his family and possessions as gifts of undeserved grace. God honored Job for his faith by restoring to him double-fold everything that he lost (Job 42:12).

Security for the future comes when a woman can commit her dreams to her only stable, trustworthy, loving guide. The Psalmist prayed, "My soul, wait thou only upon God, for my expectation is from Him" (Psalm 62:5). Freedom comes when we can honestly yield our dreams to His sovereign control, wholeheartedly trusting Him. We will discover His better will for our lives when we recognize that His plan is superior to one we could originate (Proverbs 3:5-6).

"Serve the LORD with fear and rejoice with trembling."
--Psalm 2:11

**"He will fulfill the desire of them that fear him:
he also will hear their cry and will save them."**
--Psalm 145:19

STUDY GUIDE   LESSON 5

MARY: A WOMAN WHO REVERENCES GOD

1. Read Luke 10:38-42. Mary and Martha are sisters. Both desire to please Jesus, but only one is praised. Why is Mary praised?

   ①Mary was sitting at Christ feet to hear his word. she has a desire to hear & know God's word.
   ② Christ commended her for her wisdom "She had chosen the good part."

2. Why is Martha rebuked? *for being anxious and troubled about many things. The thing she was anxious about were needless. while the one thing she did need she neglected. Her work was proper at the right time but now she had other thing to do*

3. How might Martha have been different in Luke 10:40-42 if she had taken time to listen to Jesus before she served? *see pg 30 #1-7.*
   1 Developed a confidence in God   *5. Priorities in order*
   2 " a meek & quiet spirit   *6 less judgmental of Mary*
   3. may have sought council   *7. may have been honored.*
   4. a better Hostess

4. The King James translation states that "Martha was cumbered about much serving" (Luke 10:40a). Are you ever weighed down as you serve? Why? How can you serve more like Mary? *Sometimes our lives get so busy & what we do may sometimes seem meaningless. If we take time to spend in prayer & bible reading each day we will accomplish more for christ*

5. How does Jesus describe true servanthood (Mark 10:42-45)? Would Martha's example match this concept of servanthood? Why or why not? *a true servant serves his people and does not want to be lord over them No. Martha rebuked Mary. By spending time w/ christ she would learn the service that is truly pleasing to him.*

   He that affects to be chief shall be servant of all

6. Can you think of a situation in your life where effective service came after spiritual worship?
   prayer before a task?

Note: The first part of the homework to the next lesson needs to be started the morning after finishing this class discussion. See question 1 of Lesson 6.

MARY: A WOMAN WHO REVERENCES GOD

"She rises while it is night, and gives spiritual food for her household. . .
She girds herself with **strength** *. . ."* (spiritual, mental
and physical fitness for her God given task).
—Proverbs 31:15,17 Amplified

Hair fell into her eyes and she brushed it aside as she shaped her bread cakes. She paused to wipe her hands so she could stir the lentil stew. The pilaf still needed to be made and the table arranged. Someone needed to cut up the fruit salad and pour the olives in a bowl. Where was her sister anyway? Why was she left to work in the kitchen alone?

Martha stooped to pass through the doorway to the other room. Anger raged inside her when she spotted Mary kneeling beside Jesus, listening intently to his every word.

"Lord, do You not care that my sister has left me to serve alone?" Martha asked indignantly. "Tell her to help me!" she commanded (Luke 10:40, NKJV).

Jesus turned slowly. His eyes locked with Martha in a penetrating stare. "Martha, Martha," the Lord answered, "you are worried and troubled about many things. But one thing is needed. Mary has chosen that good part which will not be taken away from her" (Luke 10:41-42, NKJV).

Mary and Martha, sisters from the town of Bethany, both desired to please the Lord. However, Jesus rebuked one woman for her effort while he praised the other. Why?

Did Jesus disapprove of servanthood? Hardly. He repeatedly taught the importance of humble service. Yet, Jesus, the supreme Servant, the one who "came not to be ministered unto, but to minister" (Mark 10:45), did not order Mary to get to work.

Our first reaction to the account might be sympathy for Martha. We've all been in situations where we were left with all the dirty work while others enjoyed themselves. Martha accused Mary of laziness and, on first appearance, we might tend to agree with her. But Jesus saw Martha's heart and motives.

Spiritual Insensitivity Produces Meaningless Service

Martha's error came from wrong priorities. Devotion needs to precede action. Service in and of itself does not necessarily have great value. Only service that is rendered for the right reasons and with a proper goal in mind is profitable. An unneeded service project consumed Martha. The purpose of Jesus coming to the sisters' home was not to be frantically served. He wanted to impart spiritual truths. Let us consider some possible changes in the Luke 10 scene if Martha had sought direction from the Lord before she served.

Possible Changes if Martha Had Worshipped First:

1. MARTHA MIGHT HAVE DEVELOPED CONFIDENCE IN GOD. She would have never implied, as she did in Luke 10:40, that Jesus was unconcerned for her best welfare. She would have known that Jesus not only cared, (1 Peter 5:7), but that he was willing to sacrifice His life in acting upon His concern.

2. MARTHA MIGHT HAVE DEVELOPED A MEEK AND QUIET SPIRIT. Face to face with the Prince of Peace and Lifter of Loads (see Psalm 68:19), Martha was weighed down with self-imposed burdens. She was "careful and troubled about many things" (Luke 10:41) when she could have claimed the peace of God (Isaiah 26:3).

3. BOSSY MARTHA MIGHT HAVE SOUGHT COUNSEL. "For who hath known the mind of the Lord? Or who hath been his counselor?" (Romans 11:34). Martha criticized Jesus instead of seeking guidance. In Luke 10:40 she rebuked Him for not directing Mary to help her serve. Later her faith was still weak. At the gravesite of her brother, Lazarus, she questioned the Lord's command to roll away the stone. As if she knew more than Jesus, she challenged His order by interjecting the complaint, "Lord, by this time he stinketh for he hath been dead four days" (John 11:39).

4. MARTHA MIGHT HAVE BEEN A BETTER HOSTESS. The thing she wanted most to provide, a special treat for her guest, was lost in the rush of the occasion. All of her efforts obtained the opposite effect of what she had hoped. When our goals are not in harmony with God's plans, the fruit of our labor is lost. One Proverb summarized the paradox: "Better is a dry morsel with quietness, than a house full of feasting [or sacrificial meals] with strife" (Proverbs 17:1 NKJV).

5. MARTHA MIGHT HAVE HAD HER PRIORITIES IN ORDER. She was concerned with details and secondary issues instead of the main priority . The greatest need was not to entertain Jesus. It was to eat of the eternal bread He would provide.

6. MARTHA MIGHT HAVE BEEN LESS JUDGMENTAL OF MARY. When we focus on the Lord, our judgmental spirit of others is changed to one filled with compassion and love. When we are out of fellowship with God we are often critical of people, even ones who are not in error.

7. MARTHA MIGHT HAVE BEEN HONORED. Jesus taught, "If anyone serves Me, let him follow Me; and where I am, there My servant will be also. If anyone serves Me, him My Father will honor." (John 12:26 NKJV).

<u>Devotion Precedes Service of Lasting Value</u>

The praise of Jesus for Mary is sharply contrasted by His evaluation of her sister, Martha. Whereas Martha will be remembered as the worried housekeeper, Mary's commendation will last for eternity.

In different passages of Scripture mentioning these two women, Mary repeatedly takes the lowly spot, sitting at Jesus' feet. She listens to Him for instruction (Luke 10:39) and seeks Him for comfort (John 11:32). While Martha continues to rebuke Him (John 11:1,39), Mary quietly observes the hand of God at work. **From spending time with Jesus, she discerns the form of service that would be truly pleasing to Him.** Six days before the Passover, in anticipation of His upcoming death and burial, she washes His feet with costly ointment and dries them with her hair (John 12:1-8).

Although others scoffed, Jesus commends Mary for her actions by saying, "Why trouble ye the woman? for she hath wrought a good work upon me" (Matthew 26:10). Jesus said, "She did it to prepare me for my burial" (Matthew 26:12). Because Mary listened to the Lord's words, she knew something even the twelve did not comprehend. She foresaw his coming death.

As a memorial to Mary, God inspired her story to be retold in three of the gospel narratives. Jesus emphasized His approval when He proclaimed, "Assuredly, I say to you, wherever this gospel is preached in the whole world, what this woman has done will also be told as a memorial to her " (Matthew 26:13, NKJV).

Whole-hearted worship guides us into acceptable service. We can, like Martha, serve God our own way, or, like Mary, we can humble ourselves and spend time at His feet seeking His guidance and strength. Then after we know His will, we can intelligently serve Him in a way that will reap eternal value. "A woman who feareth the Lord, she shall be praised (Proverbs 31:30).

God's Priceless Woman will show both characteristics (ie...servant and devoted learner). But majoring on being a Mary will produce what is needed to become the right kind of Martha.

Private Devotions for GPW

Date:_____

Passage Read: _____

Main Verses to Highlight_____

_____

Ideas that inspired me: _____

_____

_____

Personal application: _____

_____

_____

##

Date:_____

Passage Read: _____

Main Verses to Highlight_____

_____

Ideas that inspired me: _____

_____

_____

Personal application: _____

_____

_____

REVERENCING GOD

1. Be prepared to share from your private devotions this week. You may either continue your regular program or read consecutively three Psalms a day. Keep a diary each day of how much you read, a main idea that impressed you and a personal application.

   For example: Date:
   Reading:
   Main Verses:
   Ideas that inspired me:
   Personal application:

2. Many godly people in Scripture and in history had a pattern of rising early to meet with God. What purposes are there in rising early to meet with God?

   1 Samuel 1:19
   Job 1:5
   Psalm 5:3
   Psalm 59:16
   Psalm 88:13
   Psalm 143:8
   Isaiah 33:2

3. What are some benefits from nightly devotions?

   Psalm 55:17
   Psalm 63:1,6,7
   Psalm 119:55
   Psalm 119:148
   Isaiah 26:8-9

4. Can you think of other ways to grow in the Lord?

5. What are some hindrances to private devotional time (Proverbs 6:9; Psalm 66:18)? Can you think of additional hindrances?

   What are some creative ways you have overcome these hindrances?

6. Optional: Describe a time in your life when a passage of Scripture came to you for comfort or direction.

REVERENCING GOD

"Speak the things which are proper for sound doctrine....
the older women likewise, that they be reverent in behavior.
(Titus 2:1, 3 NKJV)

My first child, a red-headed son, came seven weeks early. He did not breathe without assistance and then weakly. The nurse placed him in my arms long enough for his two eyes to lock with mine and win my heart. I never saw him again. He died six hours after birth.

God answered my prayer and I conceived again. Samuel arrived three weeks early. Ten days after his birth he had lost weight to below five pounds and developed severe jaundice. Our pediatrician ordered us to rush Samuel to the children's hospital neonatal intensive care unit for a total blood transfusion.

Would he live? Panic overwhelmed me with paralyzing fear. I clutched my son on the ride to the hospital. The foothills surrounding the freeway seemed to be closing in on me. A verse flashed in my mind. **"God is our refuge and strength, a very present help in trouble. Therefore will not we fear, though the earth be removed, and though the mountains be carried into the midst of the sea."** Instantly a spiritual calm replaced anxiety. I loosened my grip on Samuel and relaxed, cradling him tenderly. "Thank you, Lord, for the joy my son has brought into my life, if only for a little while. I commit Him now to your care."

One thing puzzled me. When did I learn that verse? I had done extensive Scripture memory work, but I could not remember ever studying that passage. Days passed. Samuel recovered without needing transfusions. Life returned to normal. Then one morning as I dusted the living room, I paused and read the handwritten message written on the picture I had framed years before. *"God is our refuge and strength...."*

"That's where the verse came from!" I exclaimed.

As a student wife on a limited income, I had decorated our home on creatively combined odds and ends like a salvaged picture frame. From a Bible concordance I located a verse for the peaceful mountain scene I clipped from an old magazine. I wrote the text with Indian ink on the picture glass. In the process of copying the verse on the overlay, I had unconsciously memorized it. In my hour of need, the passage redirected my focus from my problem to my Sustainer. God's Word did not return void.

Designing inspirational decorations is just one of many ways to incorporate God's thoughts into our minds so we can reverence Him in our daily activities. "Let us cleanse ourselves from all filthiness of the flesh and spirit, perfecting holiness in the fear of [or *out of reverence for*] God" (2 Corinthians 7:1).

What are some ways to strengthen our spiritual walk?

Seek The Lord For Direction At The Start Of The Day

Many godly saints start their day with a devotional period. "Cause me to hear thy lovingkindness in the morning," David said, "for in thee do I trust. Cause me to know the way wherein I should walk; for I lift up my soul unto thee" (Psalm 143:8). Again he purposed, "My voice shalt thou hear in the morning, O Lord; in the morning will I direct my prayer unto thee, and will look up" (Psalm 5:3). **Moses, Daniel** and other saints of old recognized their need for time alone with God in the morning.

Job rose early to intercede for his children (Job 1:5), and **Hannah** and **Elkanah** rose to worship the Lord (1 Samuel 1:19). The **Psalmists** searched for direction with confidence and hope in the Word (Psalm 119:147). **David** prayed (Psalm 5:3) and praised (Psalm 59:16). **Heman** acknowledged his dependence upon God (Psalm 88:14). **Jesus** sought His Father morning by morning so that He could wisely assist those in need. "The Sovereign Lord has given me an instructed tongue, to know the word that sustains the weary. He wakens me morning by morning, wakens my ear to listen like one being taught" (Isaiah 50:4 NIV).

Meditate On The Lord At The Close Of The Day

Nightly devotions are frequently mentioned in the Word. In fact, many biblical figures such as Daniel had three regular times of special prayer and fellowship with God. David speaks not only of seeking God early (Psalm 63:1), but also of meditating on Him while he is on his bed in the nightwatches (v.6). The writer of Psalm 119 speaks of hoping in the Word in the dawning of the morning (v. 147), and meditating on the Word in the night (v. 148).

To help control the subconscious thoughts during sleeping hours, many saints make a point to have at least a brief period of Bible reading before going to bed. They can then go to sleep meditating on what they read. Sometimes, during a special trial, Christians might stay up late at night for an uninterrupted period with the Lord.

Internally Implant The Word For Constant Availability

Often in Scripture God exhorts us to meditate on His Word day and night (Joshua 1:8; Psalm 1:2, etc). Several techniques can help make meditation possible throughout the day.

1. MEMORIZE KEY SCRIPTURE PASSAGES. Prepare or buy cards with key Bible verses and leave the cards in strategic places. The memory cards can be mounted on the wall of the shower with clear contact paper, clipped to the refrigerator, or taped on the first and last page of a school notebook. Verses can be tacked to a bulletin board beside the telephone or attached to a school locker or to the bathroom mirror. We can carry a

verse in our purse to redeem time through out the day. Verses can be reviewed in odd moments, waiting for an appointment or traveling.

2. SING BIBLE PASSAGES. Put Scripture to music or sing verses that others have put to music. We are more likely to joyfully remember those words that we sing. Our God is a singing God (Zephaniah 3:17). He has put a new song in the hearts of His children. Forty times in the Old Testament the prophets mention singing. The Psalms are also filled with references to singing. "I will sing unto the LORD as long as I live; I will sing praise to my God while I have my being" (Psalm 104:33). "Sing unto him, sing psalms unto him: talk ye of all his wonderous acts" (Psalm 105:2), "Then believed they his words and sang his praise" (Psalm 106:12). "Let them sacrifice the sacrifices of thanksgiving, and declare his works with rejoicing " (Psalm 107:22). "O God, my heart is fixed; I will sing and give praise, even with my glory" (Psalm 108:1). Music is a means of expression as well as an excellent medium to reinforce truth.

Plan Special Retreats

Longer periods of prayer and meditation can be revitalizing. Occasionally take time away from the normal routine to spend extra time with the Lord. Many saints intermittently spend a day or more in prayer and fasting. A special season away from the daily rush of life is particularly helpful before making a major decision. At times of concentrated devotion, one seems more responsive to the leading of the Holy Spirit (Acts 13:2-3, 14:23).

Worship and Pray Corporately

"God is greatly to be feared in the assembly of the saints, and to be had in reverence of all those who are about him" (Psalm 89:7). Private praise and worship naturally led to corporate exaltation (Psalm 34:1-3). In addition to personal worship, join together with others of like mind for a period of worship. Christ loved the church and gave himself for it (Ephesians 5:25). Much of the New Testament is addressed collectively to believers. Isolated Christians are not a part of God's plan.

Conclusion

Jesus said, "I am the vine, ye are the branches. He that abideth in me, and I in him, the same bringeth forth much fruit: for without me ye can do nothing" (John 15:5). God's priceless woman is a woman who creatively and regularly worships God.

> *"Let all the earth fear the LORD: let all the*
> *inhabitants of the world stand in awe of him.*
> (Psalm 33:8).

MIRIAM: A WOMAN WHO SPEAKS UNKINDLY

1. Read Numbers 12:1-15. How did Miriam want others to see herself and Aaron (Numbers 12:1-2)?

2. How did God view Moses (Numbers 12:3-9)?

3. How did God view the sin of Miriam (Numbers 12:9-14; Proverbs 6:16-19; 1 Timothy 5:19-20)?

4. Why does God consider gossiping to be such a serious sin?

    Proverbs 11:9

    Proverbs 16:28

    Proverbs 17:9

    Proverbs 26:20-23

5. Can you think of a situation where you have personally been hurt by gossip?

    Can you think of a case where you have been guilty of hurting someone else by being a gossiper? What steps did you make to rectify the harm done?

6. What effect did Miriam's sin have on the others (Numbers 12:15)? How can we help stop gossip (Proverbs 14:15; 15:28; 17:27-28, and 18:13, and James 3:2-18))?

MIRIAM: A WOMAN WHO SPEAKS UNKINDLY

*"Older women likewise are to be reverent in their behavior,
not malicious gossips . . . that they may encourage
the young women. . . to be . . . kind. . . . "*
(Titus 2:3-5, NASB).

Feelings of jealousy overwhelmed her as she watched the people honor her brother. Why did he get all the attention? What had he done that was better than she could do? Were they not from the same family?

One thing was certain. Unless she could lower his position, no one would notice her. What could she use to prejudice others against him? His life was blameless. What about his wife? Moses, her brother, had married interracially. Others would not feel the same loyalty for his wife as they did for their spiritual leader.

Now to recruit assistance. Aaron fell as easy prey. He too struggled with sibling rivalry and envy over his brother's popularity. He took up Miriam's offense.

Together Miriam and Aaron challenged the people, "Has the LORD indeed spoken only through Moses? Hasn't he not spoken through us also?" (Numbers 12:2, NKJV).

Their plan failed. "And the LORD heard it" (v.2b). God knew the true character of Moses. He described him as "very humble, more humble than all men who were on the face of the earth" (v.3). The Lord called the three siblings to stand in front of the Tent of Meeting. Miriam, like a guilty child facing her father, must have felt frightened to stand before God in her sin.

The Lord exposed her error. He called her closer and said:

> *If there is a prophet among you, I, the LORD, make Myself known to him in a vision, And I speak to him in a dream. Not so with My servant Moses; He is faithful in all my house. I speak with him face to face, even plainly, and not in the dark sayings; and he sees the form of the LORD. Why then were you not afraid to speak against my servant Moses? (vv.6-9).*

The Lord's anger burned against Miriam. He graphically revealed his displeasure. When he left, the woman who sought praise stood exposed and shamed, covered with the dreadful disease of leprosy. After Moses interceded for her healing, God promised to cleanse her, but not until she suffered isolation outside the camp seven days (v.15). Her sin caused her personal embarrassment and grief, and the entire assembly suffered as well. "The people did not journey on till Miriam was brought in again" (v.15b).

The Danger of Gossip

Gossip devastates the work of the Lord.

1. GOSSIP DESTROYS FRIENDSHIPS AND DIVIDES BELIEVERS. The blade of gossip can destructively cut through even the best of friendships (Psalm 50:19-23; Proverbs 16:28). Because it is so simple to slip into this sin, and yet so devastating to the work of the Lord, victory over gossip is a prerequisite to teaching other women (Titus 2:3-5). Slander or gossip is a verbal attempt to discredit another person. But God is listening to our conversations. He will clear the innocent.

Unity of believers is so important that actions that spread discord are abominations to God (Proverbs 6:16, 19), especially accusations against those in leadership (1Timothy 5:19).

2. GOSSIP INTENSIFIES THE INITIAL PROBLEM. A woman may gossip to release the pressure mounting from an unresolved conflict. She shares private information with someone who is neither part of the conflict nor part of the solution. Hesitant to go directly to the offender, she lets off steam by telling a third party. However, instead of releasing tension, gossiping magnifies the offense. The burden grows and the basic problem remains unresolved.

A number of questions might help determine the motivation behind the temptation to gossip. We might ask: "Do I care more about a resolution to the problem, or am I enjoying thinking about the problem itself? Am I motivated by envy, pride, or selfish ambition? Do I want to expose this person so I will look better? Do I desire harmony and peace in the body of Christ, or would I be pleased with division? Am I using prayer as an excuse for gossip? If I were the person in question, would I want others talking about me in this way?"

The ministry of protecting is contrasted with the destruction of gossip in Proverbs 10:12. "Hatred stirs up strife, but love covers over all sins." When tempted to criticize someone we do well to remember "how good and how pleasant it is for brethren to dwell together in unity!" (Psalm 133:1b).

Responding to Gossip

Avoid being baited to take sides or "take up an offense". One who takes-up-an-offense is one who listens to another's complaint and becomes personally involved. Instead of directing the gossiper to return to the party in question, the one taking-up-an-offense sides with the gossiper. Yet the gossiper may leave out significant points that completely alter the meaning behind key events. A third party intensifies the problem by reinforcing the wrong felt while not being able to fill in the missing links that can ease the hurt.

The Benefits of Peacemaking

A peacemaker is one who lovingly resolves conflicts. She stops negative chain reactions. Listening to a gossiper only adds fuel to that tale bearer's fire. "For without wood the fire goes out, and where there is no whisperer, contention quiets down" (Proverbs 26:20, NASB). Instead of enjoying the "juicy story," the peacemaker will redirect the gossiper to go to the person in question. She should ask, "Why are you telling me this?" or "Have you talked to this person about your misunderstanding?" Remember that even listening to gossip can be harmful for all involved. "The words of a tale bearer are as wounds, and they go down into the innermost parts of the belly" (Proverbs 26:22).

When she overhears a negative story about a friend, the peacemaker will not jump to hasty conclusions. The Bible warns us not to make assumptions without hearing the facts (Proverbs 14:15). One side of a story is never a complete story (Proverbs 11:9; 18:13). The peacemaker may want to clarify derogatory information by later asking the person who was criticized discrete questions.

James promises that the "fruit of righteousness is sown in peace by them that make peace" (James 3:18). Gossipers hold back the work of God like Miriam held back the entire camp, but women who speak with kindness will bless others.

SPEAKING WITH KINDNESS

1. The Proverbs 31 woman spoke with wisdom and kindness (v.26). What are some positive ways we can use our tongues? Explain.

   Psalm 34:1-3 *- to praise the Lord - to exalt him*
   Proverbs 12:18b *- the wise will speak to comfort + help*
   Proverbs 12:25 *- to cheer & lift someone up - especially if from God*
   Proverbs 15:1 *- peace can be kept with kind words*
   Proverbs 16:23-24 *unless there is wisdom within the heart sweet words would only be flattery - wisdom in the heart is the main thing*

2. Give an example of someone whose speech ministered to you recently. Explain why these words were so meaningful.

3. When it is impossible or impractical to overlook an offense, why is it best to talk directly to the party involved before discussing the matter with anyone else?
   - go & talk to the person first, get all the facts right,
   Proverbs 25:9-12 *save his reputation by not telling others*
   Matthew 18:15 *- talk to him alone. you may gain a friendship rather than break one*
   Luke 17:3-4 *- if you are permitted to rebuke him do so. it may be that it was a misunderstanding - if he repents. Drop the matter*

4. How can we reprove wisely (Prov. 9:8-9, 25:15; Gal. 6:1; Eph. 4:15, and Col. 4:6)?
   when reproving; offer instruction with it. wait for a good opportunity and allow time to think about it, use a spirit of meekness, love & truth, speak in a christian manner.
   Have you ever been reproved wisely (or unwisely)? If so, describe the result .

5. Why do we flatter? Why is it wrong? *- it is deceitful*
   the Lord knows our motives + we must speak
   Proverbs 12: 2, 17-19 *in love & truth. a deceitful tongue the Lord will condemn*
   Proverbs 26:28 *- a lying tongue many people can see, but a flattery is often not suspected*
   Proverbs 29:5 *to speak good to someone when it is not true can puff up a person with pride*

6. Why do we nag? Share a recent personal illustration of nagging. How did the other person respond? *We are not content*

   Describe the effect of nagging.
   a continual pestering about something
   Proverbs 19:13b *-*
   Proverbs 21:19 *- they cannot live in peace & love with a constant nagging*
   Proverbs 25:24 *- they would rather live in a corner of the attic than in a big beautiful house*

A WOMAN WHO SPEAKS WITH KINDNESS

"She openeth her mouth with wisdom;
and in her tongue is the law of kindness."
(Proverbs 31:26)

Karen listened intently as her husband Bob taught the adult Sunday School class. She longed for him to be a strong leader and determined to help him excel. "He's so fortunate to have me," she thought proudly. "How else would he realize how many ways he could improve?"

One Sunday afternoon before Karen had presented her critique of the morning's lesson, Bob confessed, "I think I should resign from teaching next month."

"Resign???" Karen echoed, her voice reflecting her confusion. "Who could take YOUR place? You're an outstanding teacher."

Bob looked at his feet. "How could I be when I make so many mistakes?" he asked.

"But your errors are all minor," Karen assured him. He raised his head. A hint of life returned to his eyes. For the first time she understood how she had destroyed his self-esteem in her effort to help. The next week she chose a new approach. She decided to mentally note all the things her husband did right. She prayed and asked God to help her be an honest encourager. After class she casually spoke. "Larry really asked a difficult question today. I wondered how I would have responded." Bob displayed no interest in the discussion, but she continued. "Boy, you handled that one well!"

Bob stared at Karen in disbelief. He questioned, a hint of pleasure in his voice, "Did I really?"

His look begged for more, so Karen continued to praise several other specific strong points of the day's lesson. He smiled and listened intently. Week after week she continued to build him up. After she stopped nagging, he, in time, overcame long-time areas of weakness. As she continued to uphold him, his leadership abilities grew. Several years later he entered full-time Christian service.

The same tongue that can be "an unruly evil, full of deadly poison" (James 3:8), can minister to others. **Right words are compared to the sweetness of honeycomb, healing to the bones and precious jewels** (Proverbs 16:23,24).

In this study we want to investigate some of the ways we can edify or uplift others with our speech. Conversely, we will consider forms of speech which are destructive and need to be avoided. The priceless woman should learn to protect friends, promote peace, and praise others.

Wholesome Speech

Ephesians 4:29-32 describes several ways we can guard others by controlling our speech.

1. BE SENSIBLE AND DISCRETE. A godly woman's speech should edify. "Do not let any unwholesome talk come out of your mouths, but only what is helpful for building others up according to their needs, that it may benefit those who listen" (v. 29, NIV). Guard other people's time by avoiding trivial conversations. Women are known offenders for excessive chatter (Ecclesiastes 5:3b).

Pure speech protects the listener. Speaking openly about sexual sins, even in a condemning way, can arouse lustful desires. Such things should not even be named (Ephesians 5:3-4; 11-12).

2. BE MOTIVATED BY LOVE. "Let all bitterness, and wrath, and anger, and clamour, and evil speaking, be put away from you, with all malice" (Ephesians 4:31). Replace animosity with mercy and love. "And be ye kind one to another, tenderhearted, forgiving one another, even as God for Christ's sake hath forgiven you" (v.32).

One with a forgiving heart can overlook an offense. ("...a faithful spirit concealeth the matter"—Proverbs 11:13). **"He who covers over a transgression seeks love, but he who repeats a matter separates the best of friends"** (Proverbs 17:9, NKJV).

Sometimes, however, it is not always advisable to ignore an offense. If we feel a compulsion to talk about the problem, we need to go directly to the one involved and talk in private (Matthew 18:15; Luke 17:3-4).

> "Debate thy cause with thy neighbor himself; and discover not a secret to another; Lest he that heareth it put thee to shame, and thine infamy turn not away" (Proverbs 25:9-10).

If the offender learns that one talked behind her back, she will be hurt and find it difficult to forgive. However, if approached directly in the right spirit, the offender could be won as a friend. "As an earring of gold, and an ornament of fine gold, so is a wise reprover upon an obedient ear" (v. 12).

What is a wise reprover? A wise reprover is one willing to speak the truth in love when it has the potential of constructively helping an individual (Proverbs 9:7-9; Ephesians 4:15). She is gentle and humble (Colossians 4:6; Galatians 6:1). A mild rebuke is often adequate to produce major changes. "A gentle tongue can break a bone" (Proverbs 25:15), whereas a harsh word can produce irreparable damage.

Uplifting Speech

People are bombarded daily with criticism and rebuke. How we all long for a good word of praise. The woman who knows how to properly praise inspires those around her to grow to a fuller potential than otherwise possible. Her confidence gives them hope. They are spurred on toward love and good deeds (Hebrews 10:24) in areas they might not have attempted without encouragement from another.

No one is perfect and if we want to find things to criticize we will never have a shortage. The wise woman concentrates her efforts in overcoming her own problems. She will not waste all her energies trying to discover everyone else's faults so she will not feel as bad about her own failings. The Lord challenges, "How can you say to your brother, Let me remove the speck out of your eye; and look, a plank is in your own eye?" (Matthew 7:4, NKJV).

Each of us is exhorted to become a woman with a meek and quiet spirit (1 Peter 3:4). Our responsibility is to allow God to change us, not for us to change others. **When we concentrate on our own faults, we are more accepting of the weaknesses of others. If we focus on the positive qualities in others (Philippians 4:8), it will be natural to praise.**

1. PRAISE BUT DO NOT FLATTER. Sincere appreciation or admiration is praise but insincere compliments are flattery. One who flatters is double-hearted (Psalm 12:2), a woman who manipulates people.

Although we should avoid dishonest compliments, we should praise as frequently as possible. A meaningful compliment deals with character qualities. For example, it is better to tell a child he has a nice smile (something which he controls) than to marvel at the color of his eyes (something he has no control over).

2. ENCOURAGE BUT DO NOT NAG. To nag is to repeatedly remind one of his responsibility or constantly make sarcastic statements in an "I told you so" manner. Wives and mothers are prime offenders. Yet, nagging rarely inspires change. Even when it produces some response (most people will do anything to shut off a "leaky faucet") the changes are at best temporary. Nagging causes conflict and tension. A nagging woman is compared to constant dripping (Proverbs 19:13). A home in the wilderness is better than living with contention (Proverbs 21:19). Dwelling in the poorest of locations surpasses life in a large mansion with a brawling woman (Proverbs 25:24).

One wife learned the secret to correct her nagging spirit. Her husband always threw his pants across the chair. She repeatedly explained to him all the reasons his sloppiness bothered her. He stubbornly continued to fling his clothes over the furniture. She complained. He persisted.

During a visit from her out-of-town mother, Donna became especially angry at the sight of her husband's pants drooped over the chair. She seethed inside. Her widowed mother, who saw the trousers at the same time, shocked her daughter by responding: "Look at that. I bet you thank God that you have a husband who can throw his pants across the chair."

Donna realized she had focused on her problems and not her blessings. She decided to listen to her mother and start thanking God for a husband every time she hung his pants. When her spirit changed, her husband recognized how inconsiderate he had been and started to hang his pants instead of throwing them down at night. Actually it no longer mattered to her. The source of irritation had become a reminder of her love for him.

Steps for Gaining Tongue Control

There are two basic reasons a woman uses her tongue incorrectly. She may be offending unintentionally, or she may purposefully misuse her tongue. The first reason is ignorance. She may desire to help, but instead thwarts others by nagging or gossiping (in the form of prayer requests perhaps?). In a desire to show appreciation she may give false hope through flattery. Rather than encourage or comfort, she might talk too much. In an attempt to bear the burdens of others she may unintentionally increase their conflict by listening to gossip.

The more difficult problems to correct are those motivated by pride. One with a judgmental or envious spirit is vulnerable to gossip and taking up offenses (James 3:16). Flattery frequently comes from a woman who desires to control others. A self-righteous feeling of superiority can lead to nagging. Regardless of the root cause, however, a number of steps can be taken to gain control over the tongue.

1. RECOGNIZE THE SIN FOR WHAT IT IS. Agree with God when "helpful criticism" is really nagging, or when a "prayer request" is disguised gossip. Admit to God that listening to gossip is encouraging negative thought patterns.

2. STUDY THE CONSEQUENCES OF THE OFFENSE. For example, gossiping and the pride that inspires it are two of the seven abominable sins (Proverbs 6:16-19). God goes so far as to say that a proud heart will not be tolerated. If someone slanders her neighbor she will be punished (Psalm 101:5).

3. FOCUS ON THE CHARACTER OF GOD. Viewing God's mercy and lovingkindness helps prevent gossip. Recognizing His perfect justice counters taking sides with a gossiper. An acceptance of the sovereignty of God eliminates some of the need to nag. Flattery is less likely to be employed in view of God's perfect truthfulness. Spending time in the Word focusing on the attributes of God and truth about His character will help improve the value of our speech.

4. MAKE RESTITUTION WHEN POSSIBLE. A woman whose name has been slandered deserves an apology. Others who heard gossip should have false concepts corrected. Apologies are appropriate for a husband or children who have been nagged or a friend who has been encouraged to gossip.

5. TAKE INITIATIVE IN ASKING MEANINGFUL QUESTIONS. Guide conversations into profitable topics. Goals in life, good books read, answers to prayer, or even personal testimonies are edifying subjects. Ask older women for advice regarding key areas of life. Try to build others up. Praise whenever you can do so sincerely. Be positive. Develop a thankful spirit (Ephesians 5:4). A demolition crew can tear down a house in a few hours. Building up takes much longer.

6. KEEP CONSTRUCTIVELY BUSY. Idleness is often related to improper speech. "For we hear," reports Paul, "that there are some who walk among you disorderly, working not at all, but are busybodies (2 Thessalonians 3:11). Again he warns, "they learn to be idle, wandering about from house to house; not only idle but tattlers also and busybodies, speaking things which they ought not" (1 Timothy 5:13). Industry, creativity and resourcefulness help counter tongue problems.

7. MEMORIZE VERSES RELATED TO VICTORY IN THE SPECIFIC AREA. A woman who desires to minister to other women, for example, might claim Titus 2:3-5. She will recognize that in order to work effectively with others she must gain control over gossiping. Visualizing this goal helps create the incentive to guard the tongue.

8. DEVELOP A DEEP DEVOTIONAL TIME. Tongue control will only be complete when a woman is able to "bless the Lord at all times." Time in the Word helps reveal one's own "secret faults" as well as "presumptuous sins." It is after desiring the riches of the Bible more than the value of fine gold that one can say, "I shall be innocent from the great transgression. Let the words of my mouth, and the meditation of my heart, be acceptable in thy sight, O Lord, my strength, and my redeemer" (Psalm 19:12-14).

Conclusion

People are sensitive. A small comment can sting painfully or uplift gloriously. "Death and life are in the power of the tongue: and they that love it shall eat the fruit thereof" (Proverbs 18:21). "**Encouragement is awesome**," explains Charles R. Swindoll. "Think about it: **It has the capacity to lift a man's or woman's shoulders. To spark the flicker of a smile on the face of a discouraged child. To actually change the course of another human being's day...or week...or life.**" [1]

---

1 Swindoll, Charles R. Encourage Me: Caring Words for Heavy Hearts (Multnomah Press: 1982) p.85. Used by permission.

QUEEN ESTHER: A WOMAN OF SELF-CONTROL
Queen Esther positively models self-control.
For background read Esther chapters 1-7
and then answer the following questions.

1. Describe King Ahasuerus (Xerxes).

    Describe Esther (2:7, 9).

2. Do you believe there is a connection between her maturity in responding to wise
    counsel and her fruit of self-control?   Explain (Esther 2: 10,15,20).

3. In what ways did Esther model victory over self-gratification (Esther 4:11-17)?

4. How did she exemplify control over her tongue (Esther 5:1-8; 7:1-6)?

5. What actions did Esther take to ensure self-control (Esther 5:1-8; 7:1-6)?

6. What benefits came out of her victory? How did her self-control help others?

QUEEN ESTHER: A WOMAN OF SELF-CONTROL

*"The heart of her husband safely trusts her;
so he will have no lack of gain"*
(Proverbs 31:11 NKJV).

She married an abusive, tyrannical man, a chauvinist with a vicious temper. He mistreated his first wife and now his affection for her had waned. She urgently needed to appeal for his help, but could she do so successfully?

Queen Esther, heroine of the Old Testament book bearing her name, married King Ahasuerus, a temperamental man. For an offense, he removed his lovely first queen, Vashti. Beautiful Esther replaced the deposed queen because "the king loved Esther above all the women, and she obtained grace and favour in his sight more than all the virgins" (Esther 2:17).

Not knowing the Queen was a Jew, Haman, a brilliant, ruthless, ambitious leader in the king's court manipulated a decree to kill all Jews—men, women and children. Esther's cousin, Mordecai, who had also been her guardian, urged her to plea for her people. But the king's fancy for lovely Queen Esther was fading (he had not called for her in thirty days) and anyone who entered the king's court without being summoned could be executed at once. The historian Josephus explained that men standing around the king's throne held axes ready to punish those who approached the king unbidden. The only hope for leniency was if the king held out his golden scepter. [1]

Mordecai reminded Esther of the consequences of not acting. The lives of a nation of people were at stake. He added, "Who knoweth whether thou art come to the kingdom for such a time as this?" (Esther 4:14).

Esther Models Self-Restraint

In her hour of testing Esther demonstrates restraint over self.

1. ESTHER DID NOT ALLOW HER FLESHLY DESIRES TO CONTROL HER. She wisely responded to her guardian's challenge by appealing for help. "Go gather together all the Jews that are present in Shushan, and fast ye for me, and neither eat nor drink three days, night or day".

Then she shared her personal plans. "I also and my maidens will fast likewise; and so will I go unto the king, which is not according to the law: and if I perish, I perish" (Esther 4:16). Out of love for her people she was willing to control her natural desire for food and water and sacrificially risk her life.

2. ESTHER DID NOT SPEAK IMPULSIVELY. Another example of self-restraint is her patience in waiting for the right moment to appeal to the king. She appeared unannounced to Ahasuerus. After much suspense, he received his bride. He not only extended the golden scepter of recognition, but he also responded positively. "What wilt thou, Queen Esther? and what is thy request?" He called her by her title as queen as well as by her first name, indicating that he was in a responsive, giving mood. Most impulsive women would jump at this chance to announce the mission. Instead, she invited him to bring Haman to a dinner which she, by faith, had already prepared. Perhaps she sensed the need for privacy from the court.

At the banquet, in the presence of Haman, the king repeated his offer to the queen. Esther, in a quiet, deliberate manner invited the two state leaders to another meal the next day. In light of the urgency of her mission, we can marvel at her Spirit-led-self-control. Her postponement of the secret petition showed extraordinary wisdom. The extra time with the king helped rebuild his affections as well as stimulate his curiosity. Surely she risked her life for some important reason, or so the king must have reasoned. The extra twenty-four hours produced key events which paved the way for the overwhelming change of events: Haman was humiliated, Mordecai honored, and the Jewish nation saved.

Principles of Self-Control in Queen Esther

Instead of being the nagging wife, the kind shown as a constant dripping (Proverbs 27:15 NIV), or a woman overcome with gluttony, Esther demonstrated self-control in her speech and in her actions. Principles from her experience can be helpful to the modern-day woman, whatever her particular weak area.

1. SELF-CONTROL IS AIDED BY SUBMISSION TO PROVEN GODLY COUNSEL. Yielding self to wise advice prepares one for yielding self-desire to the will of God. Even after she became queen, Esther "obeyed the command of Mordecai as when she was brought up by him" (Esther 2:20 NKJV). **Unlike many head-strong young women, Esther sought and respected the wisdom of others older and wiser than herself.** She won the favor of Hegai by her teachable spirit (Esther 2:8,9). When it was her turn to be presented to the king as a prospective queen, she "asked for nothing other than what Hegai, the king's eunuch who was in charge of the harem, suggested. And Esther won the favor of everyone who saw her" (Esther 2:15).

2. SELF-CONTROL NEEDS TO BE IN ACCORD WITH GOD'S REVEALED PUR-POSES. God has a special plan for the nation of Israel. Mordecai reminded Esther of God's promised plan for the Jews. If she refused to be the vessel of service, God would still preserve His people, but her father's house would be destroyed (Esther 4:14). The assurance of being in harmony with God's ultimate purposes gave her a godly boldness when necessary.

3. SELF-CONTROL IS REINFORCED BY DILIGENT PRAYER. Esther recognized her own inability to face the difficult king. She needed empowerment from God and prayer support from others (Esther 4:16).

4. SELF-CONTROL IS AIDED BY PREPLANNED STEPS OF ACTION. Esther prepared the banquet before she went to her husband-king (Esther 5:4). This action helped her resist the natural temptation to blurt out everything before he was ready to receive her request. She planned ahead so she might be able to succeed.

5. SELF-CONTROL CANNOT BE LEGISLATED, but must be Spirit-led. Christians do not live under the law but under grace. Many areas cannot be prescribed for others. Esther, led by the Spirit in her specific circumstances, delayed confronting the king. Areas of personal conviction must come from individualized Spirit-led application.

Esther heroically averted mass murder of her people. The benefits of Esther's self-control extended to her family and friends. Today, thousands of years later, the Jews still commemorate her feat in an annual celebration called Purim.

---

1 Whiston, William (translated from original Greek). The Works of Flavius Josephus: Antiquities of the Jews: A History of the Jewish Wars (Hartford, Conn: The S.S.Scranton Co., 1905) p.341.

STUDY GUIDE   LESSON 10

GAINING SELF-CONTROL

1. Define self-control. Galatians 5:22-25 might help you write a definition.

2. Titus 2:3 instructs a mature Christian woman to not be addicted to anything like wine. Why is self-control a requirement for training others?

3. Although wine, in itself, is not necessarily bad (Psalm 104: 15; 1 Timothy 5:23), enslavement to wine is one example of loss of control. What are some reasons to avoid excessive drinking?

    Proverbs 23:20-21
    Proverbs 23:29-35
    Isaiah 28:7
    Philippians 3:18-19
    1 Peter 4:7 (see NIV)

    Can you name other areas that might entangle a woman's life?

4. Ultimately what should be the Christian's motivation for self-control? (Romans 13:10-14; Romans 14:21; 1 Corinthians 10:31; 2 Corinthians 5:9).

5. Contrast Proverbs 24:13 and Proverbs 25:16,27 and explain how some things which are good in themselves can be bad by misuse.

6. Select an area in your life where you desire greater spirit- control. List two or more specific "do able" actions that will help you reach that goal.

    Desired goal:

    Action needed:

    Action needed:

GAINING SELF-CONTROL

"Not given to much wine. . . that they may teach the young women
to be sober . . . to be discreet [or self-controlled]"
(Titus 2:3-5).

Terry was 60 pounds overweight, unhappy, angry and trapped. She agonized at being fat, but continued eating and going on food binges **until...**

Jane tried to stop yelling at her children. She knew her angry tone antagonized them, and yet she could not control her tongue **until...**

Marsha battled guilt, shame, remorse, but she felt so lonely, so starved for affection, she could not sever the immoral relationship until she learned the secret to self-control.

Many like these women are enslaved to sin and can identify with Paul in grieving, "I have the desire to do what is good, but I cannot carry it out. For what I do is not the good I want to do; no the evil I do not want to do—this I keep on doing" (Romans 7:18b-19 NIV). But Paul discovers that deliverance from fleshly desires is possible (Romans 7:24-25). Later Paul includes this supernatural control-over-self as a qualification for women who aspire to train others (Titus 2:3-5).

Self-Control Defined

Self-control is the ability to say "no", to stop at a proper time, to moderate activities, to regulate facilities, passions and appetites by using sound judgment and a conscience enlightened by the Holy Spirit. A Spirit-empowered fruit, self-control is the last of nine Christian virtues listed in Galatians 5:22-23. The opposite is seen in such things as immorality, strife, anger, drunkenness and things like these (Galatians 5:19-21). Because Christ crucified the flesh, a Christian can claim the freedom to be God-directed rather than overcome by fleshly forces.

1. AREAS NEEDING CONTROL. Though often referring specifically to moderation or abstinence from alcohol, self-control is a broad term. Anything that conflicts with sensible, Spirit-led living is a threat to one's control-over-self. Modern-day habit-forming items like drugs, tranquilizers, or cigarettes have much the same destructive effects as enslavement to wine. In a lesser degree, items like caffeine and refined sugar have a similar addictive nature that, for many, is overpowering. Other areas needing control include such things as money, speech, emotions, thoughts, food, time usage, friendships, sexuality and pastime activities.

2. WAYS TO GAUGE SELF-CONTROL. One way to test an activity is to ask: "Who is in control, the Spirit or my flesh?" (1 Corinthians 6:12). "Is there a conflict between the two?" "What is the result?" Does it build up or tear down? (1 Corinthians 10:23). "Am

I enslaved? Does this activity overshadow my ability to be sensible?" If the flesh is in control the body will be defiled. "For they that are after the flesh do mind the things of the flesh; but they that are after the Spirit, the things of the Spirit. For to be carnally minded is death; but to be spiritually minded is life and peace. Because the carnal mind is enmity against God: for it is not subjected to the law of God, neither indeed can be. So then they that are in the flesh cannot please God" (Romans 8:5-8).

Each individual must determine her own degree of conviction in non-essential areas of doctrine. For example, the Bible does not command total abstinence from wine. Moderation is required, but abstinence, though commended (Proverbs 31:4-5), is not explicitly demanded of everyone (Proverbs 31:6).

Eating is another area of personal choice. Foods created by God are essential to life, but a person can either eat poor quality food or eat excessively, thereby changing the life-giving endeavor to a life-harming procedure. Honey, a healthy food when eaten in moderation, is an excellent demonstration of how something good can be misused. **"My son, eat honey,"** advised King Solomon, **"because it is good, and the honeycomb which is sweet to your taste"** (Proverbs 24:13, NKJV). But he warns, "Have you found honey? Eat only as much as you need, lest you be filled with it and vomit. . . . **It is not good to eat too much honey** " (Proverbs 25:16,27, NKJV).

Self-control should be carefully monitored by the Holy Spirit. "Happy is he who does not condemn himself in what he approves. But he who doubts is condemned if he eats, because he does not eat from faith; for whatever is not from faith is sin" (Romans 14:22b-23, NKJV).

The Benefits of Self-Control

Self-control produces long-term rewards, but lack of control brings regrets. The example of Esau is given in Scripture as a warning. For one morsel of lentil soup he sold his birthright, but afterward he sorrowfully regretted this impulsive decision (Hebrews 12:16-17).

1. SELF-CONTROL BRINGS PERSONAL FREEDOM. Lack of control in a given area usually leads to loss whereas self-control makes true fulfillment possible. Consider specific trouble areas.

    a. Money. Control over spending provides financial freedom, but lack of control means "the borrower is a servant to the lender" (Proverbs 22:7).

    b. Emotions. The woman who rules over her spirit experiences peace, but the individual controlled by strong emotional outbursts ensnares her soul (Proverbs 22:24-25).

c. **Speech**. The woman who can refrain from telling all she knows keeps her soul from troubles. (Proverbs 21:23).

d. **Sex**. A chaste woman protects herself from many hurts. The woman who commits sexual sin destroys herself. In this life her shame will never be wiped away (Proverbs 6:32-33).

e. **Eating/Drinking**. The woman who can control her eating and drinking habits improves her health and increases her vitality. She feels better about herself and toward God. In contrast, addiction to things like wine can become an all-consuming destructive drive (Isaiah 5:11-13a).

2. SELF-CONTROL IN ONE AREA FREES ONE TO DEVELOP CONTROL IN OTHER AREAS. Over-indulgence to wine, for example, affects many aspects of life. The woman given to much wine may neglect her family or be more prone to immorality. Her temper may be more likely to flare up (Romans 13:13) and her financial freedom may be jeopardized (Proverbs 21:17). Worst of all, the Lord is pushed to the wayside (Hosea 7:14).

A variety of troubles can come from enslavement to addictive forces (Proverbs 23:29-35). Lack of control over eating left the Old Testament priest, Eli, incapable of properly training his sons. Patterning after their father's gluttony (1 Samuel 2:29), they fell into immorality (1 Samuel 2:22). The Lord judged Eli's house "forever for the iniquity which he knoweth; because his sons made themselves vile, and he restrained them not" (1 Samuel 3:13).

3. SELF-CONTROL AIDS DECISION-MAKING. Enslavement to fleshly desires confuses one's thinking. "Through strong drink, they err in vision, they stumble in judgment" (Isaiah 28:7). "Wine is a mocker, strong drink is raging: and whoever is deceived thereby is not wise (Proverbs 20:1).

The Holy Spirit indicates the necessity of self-control as a quality for one who trains others (1 Timothy 3:3,8,11). Instead of being dominated by human desires, the trainer's major concern should be the will of God. With a clear mind she can pray and minister to others (1 Peter 34:2,7).

<u>Steps to Achieving Self-Control</u>

1. LEARN TO VIEW TEMPTATION THE WAY GOD DOES. Trust God's desire for our benefit. Focus on averted consequences rather than missed pleasure. For example, Neva Coyle, founder of Overeaters Victorious, explained how she stopped looking at certain foods as rewards. "Things like candy and ice cream," she exclaimed, "are no friends of mine. They aren't treats, either, I'll tell you that. They are enemies. I don't consider cake and cookies refreshment either. Not when I was once 248 pounds. These

foods are threats to my health and well-being. I choose to stand firm and not be subject again to the yoke of slavery these kinds of refreshments and treats once had on me. My treats are now healthy, life-giving foods, the kind my body loves."[1]

2. AVOID BONDAGE TO MAN-MADE LAWS. Do not erect impossible lists of laws to follow. Self-made religion, self-abasement or severe treatment of the body does not conquer fleshly indulgence (Colossians 2:20-23). Our focus should be on the Lord of glory (Colossians 3:1 ff).

3. DEVELOP A SPIRITUAL MOTIVE FOR VICTORY. The most powerful motivation to live wisely is to please the Lord. Terry found that the desire to look nice was not a strong enough motive to conquer her gluttony. She realized that selfishness motivated her over-eating. Self-gratification in one area (praise for a trim figure), could not overpower another fleshly desire (the urge to eat). She recognized that her compulsive eating stemmed from a spiritual problem. She had looked to food as a source of meeting needs — an outlet for ventilating anger, frustration and jealousy.

Not until her motives changed could she maintain her ideal weight. She learned to turn to God to fulfill her desires, claiming: **"Delight thyself also in the Lord: and he shall give thee the desires of thine heart"** (Psalm 37:4). Being motivated to please Him, she learned to use food instead of having it use her. She not only lost 60 pounds and kept it off, but she learned to control selfish impulses. Her relationships with other people improved dramatically as well.

The proper motivation to live wisely is to please the Lord. Christians are compared with soldiers and athletes who concentrate their efforts on being fit for competition. In Philippians 3:14 Paul speaks of pressing for the goal to win the future prize much the way a star runner invests all her energies to win a race. He challenges Christians to follow his example of wholehearted commitment to the Lord, instead of patterning after those whose destiny is destruction, whose god is their stomach and whose glory is their shame (Philippians 3:19).

4. MAKE NO PROVISIONS FOR THE FLESH. The person desiring self-control should purpose to resist temptation in areas of particular vulnerability. A woman prone to over drink will need to avoid stocking her pantry with wine. A glutton may need to be certain to eat before shopping for groceries. A compulsive spender might need to destroy or cancel her credit cards and learn to pray for at least twenty-four hours before making an unplanned purchase. A woman vulnerable to sexual temptation needs to be cautious about reading material. A woman hypnotized by television or some other time waster may need to sell her set while seeking to stimulate new areas of growth.

5. POSITIVELY FILL THE VOID LEFT BY NEW LIFE DISCIPLINES.Prayer and Bible study can produce a spiritual "high" that does not give a hangover. One woman who victoriously overcame a life-time struggle claims much of her power for victory came from diligent time in prayer and Scripture memory. Literally she obeyed the

Biblical counsel of Ephesians 5:17-18: "Wherefore be ye not unwise, but understanding what the will of the Lord is. And be not drunk with wine, wherein is excess: but be filled with the Spirit."

6. LIST GOALS AND DESIRED ACTIONS FOR ACHIEVING THEM. Tangible goals, like achieving ideal weight, need measurable activities that will help reach that goal. For example:

Desired goal: Weight loss/return to normal weight

Desired action might include:

    a. Avoid all devitalized foods with empty calories.
    b. Begin aerobics exercise program to help burn unwanted fat.
    c. Read the Word when feeling tempted to overeat.
    d. Say "NO!" to well-meaning friends who insist that breaking
       my diet once won't hurt.
    e. Drink lots of cold water.

Desired goal: Victory over temptation to yell at the children.

Desired action might include:

    a. Spend special time of prayer for each child daily.
    b. Teach instant obedience instead of obedience after loud threats.
    c. Watch diet for adequate calcium, magnesium, and B-complex
       vitamins needed for healthy nerves.
    d. Evaluate schedule to insure ample sleep and occasional breaks
       away from the children.

Desired goal: Pure thought life

Desired action might include:

    a. Evaluate reading, viewing matter—eliminating sources
       that exalt impurity and replace with new, edifying materials.
    b. Eliminate some of the over rich foods from diet—fleshly
       indulgence in one area triggers lack of control in others.
    c. Study verses in Bible on God's love for me and my completion in
       Him. Memorize Psalm 73:25, and Isaiah 40:11.
    d. Redirect energy to constructive projects. Volunteer to help a
       woman with her small children.

Conclusion

A woman who has no rule over her spirit, or in other words lacks self-control, is like a city whose walls are broken down (Proverbs 25:28). On the other hand, a woman who has developed the fruit of self-control recognizes that her body is not her own, but the temple of the Holy Spirit. She desires to honor the One who died for her by glorifying the Lord in her body and in her spirit which are God's (1 Corinthians 6:19-20). This woman of excellence has claimed the principle of 1 Corinthians 10:31 as one of her life mottos: **"Whether therefore ye eat, or drink, or whatsoever ye do, do all to the glory of God".**

---

1 Chapian, Marie. <u>Free to Be Thin</u>. (Bethany House Publishers: Minneapolis, Minnesota, 1979) p. 155. Used with permission.

EVE: A WOMAN WHO SET A BAD EXAMPLE

1. Read Genesis 1:27-28; 2:15-25; 3:1-24 as background for the following questions. Describe Eve (before the fall) in her relationship with God, Adam and her home.

   Was there a difference in God-given roles at creation? Explain.

2. Who sinned first, Adam or Eve (Genesis 3:9-19)? Who was held accountable for sin entering the world (Romans 5:12; 1 Corinthians 15:21-22)? Why? (1 Timothy 2:13-14).

   What was the difference between the original command given to Adam (Genesis 2:16-17) and Eve's understanding of the command (Genesis 3:2-3)?

   Name the ways Adam sinned.

3. What was the result of the entrance of sin into the world for:

   the woman (Genesis 3:16)

   the man (Genesis 3:17-19)

   How did the curse relate to the various role areas?

4. If the woman was designed by God to be under the protective leadership of her husband, how did having a man rule over her become a curse?

5. Is sorrow in bringing forth children limited to labor pains at birth? In what other ways would motherhood have been different without the sin nature?

6. How is your example affecting those in leadership over you? under you? other women observing your life?

EVE: A WOMAN WHO SET A BAD EXAMPLE

"Her husband is known in the gates,
when he sitteth among the elders of the land"
(Proverbs 31:23).

She had it all: a lovely home set in a scenic garden, a beautiful appearance (perfect measurements and skin fresh and new like a baby's), and a strong, intelligent, handsome, spiritually minded husband who adored her.

What can we learn from the first woman's example? Did she, like the Proverbs 31 woman, help strengthen her husband's leadership potential? Did she, like the Titus 2 model, demonstrate how to love a mate? Did she improve the world for the benefit of those who would follow?

The Serpent (Satan in disguise) deceived Eve. He offered her an "improvement" to God's plan and we've all suffered since. In the beginning God created Adam and Eve. He called them "man." **Both male and female share the image of God. No value distinction separates the two.** He created them as equals. Together as husband and wife they were considered one flesh and one body. Together they were given dominion over the animals (Genesis 1:26,27).

Although God created Adam and Eve equal in nature, he fashioned the two sexes for distinct functions and roles. The Lord created Adam first and gave to him practical and spiritual oversight.

> *And the LORD God took the man, and put him into the garden of Eden to dress it and to keep it, and the LORD God commanded the man, saying, Of every tree of the garden thou mayest freely eat: but of the tree of knowledge of good and evil, thou shalt not eat of it; for in the day that thou eatest thereof thou shalt surely die. And the LORD God said, It is not good that the man should be alone*
>
> (Genesis 2:15-18a).

God had Adam name all cattle, fowl of the air and beast of the field (Genesis 2:20). Then God created Eve as Adam's helper, encourager, supporter, and companion. She was to complete the man and help him fill his God-given role physically, intellectually, emotionally, and spiritually. Together they would replenish and subdue the earth.

Eve, the first feminist, stepped out of her circle of protection and usurped the authority from man. Adam, in turn, swayed by emotions for his wife, abdicated his leadership. Immediately the areas important to them were affected. Eve's role as mother and wife and Adam's role as leader and provider would become difficult.

The consequences of the fall include:

1. MULTIPLIED SORROW WITH CONCEPTION. To the woman God said, "I will greatly multiply thy sorrow and thy conception; in sorrow thou shalt bring forth children " (Genesis 3:16a). The difficulties of motherhood would extend beyond physical labor pains the day of a child's birth. The woman will contend with the consequences of sin on her children—rebellion, sickness or death. The potential joy of motherhood would be tainted by the fall.

2. AN UNWARRANTED DESIRE IN THE WOMAN TO RULE OVER THE MAN. The curse stated, "Thy desire shall be to thy husband, and he shall rule over you" (Genesis 3:16b). In the original Hebrew "desire" may mean "to control or overpower," as in Genesis 4:7 where sin desired to have Cain and control him. After the fall the woman battled two natures, the God-given need to reverence and submit to the man and a conflicting rebellious, self-assertive nature which makes her long to usurp his authority. The two opposing forces can make a woman fight to have the reins in a marriage but then hate the husband if he gives in to her.

3. A SINFUL HUSBAND TO RULE OVER A SINFUL WIFE. "He shall rule over you," (Genesis 3:16b). The curse given to Eve was not submission, since headship was established at creation. Now fallen man would rule over her. He would no longer rule perfectly. Instead of having her best interests at heart, loving and caring for her needs above his own, his leadership would be tainted by selfishness and chauvinism, or the false idea that he is superior to the woman.

4. TOIL IN CULTIVATING THE GROUND. The curse for the man was not work in itself. At creation God told him to subdue the earth and tend the garden (Genesis 2:15). The curse was the increased burden of working hardened, thorn-infested ground. Being breadwinner would not bring the unhindered joy available before the fall (Genesis 3:17-18).

5. PHYSICAL AND SPIRITUAL DEATH. Man had been forewarned that sin would result in death (Genesis 2:17). God had to pronounce the judgment, "dust thou art and unto dust shalt thou return" (Genesis 3:19). As the spiritual leader, and the first to sin with full knowledge of his actions (1 Timothy 2:13-14), Adam passed on his sin nature to all his descendants (Romans 5:12-19), and with it the curse of mortal bodies.

Need to Encourage Male Leadership Today

The scene at creation explains why God commands a woman not to teach or usurp authority over man (1 Timothy 2:11-14). Two points are mentioned. The first deals with the order of creation. The second deals with the difference in nature. The woman can be easily deceived.

Eve exemplifies the woman's susceptibility to deception. The serpent beguiled Eve and took advantage of her imprecise understanding of God's Word. The Lord had commanded Adam, "Of every tree of the garden thou mayest freely eat: but of the tree of the knowledge of good and evil, thou shalt not eat of it: for in the day that thou eatest thereof thou shalt surely die" (Genesis 2:16-17).

Eve's understanding of the command was inaccurate in three ways. First, **she underplayed the goodness of the blessing.** God had offered, "You may eat freely." Eve quoted Him as saying simply, "we may eat" (Genesis 3:2). Secondly, **she exaggerated the prohibition.** To the command to not eat the forbidden fruit she added the restriction, "neither shall ye touch it" (Genesis 3:3). Lastly, **she minimized the punishment.** She made God's proclaimed penalty only a probable consequence. Eve quoted God's warning as being, "lest ye die" (Genesis 3:3), instead of the emphatic, "You will surely die" (Genesis 2:17). She was tricked into doubting the goodness of God and the penalty of sin.

<u>Exceptions Considered</u>

Some say the Bible does not oppose female leadership over men in the church. They use Deborah as an example. However the days of the Judges were not normative. The times were characterized by everyone doing that which was right in their own eyes (Judges 17:6;21:25), a day of national weakness and decay. The Bible says Deborah "was leading Israel" (Judges 4:4), but she did not judge in the temple. No man led. People came to her under a palm tree. The Bible does not say that God raised her up as it does of the other judges (Judges 3:9,15; 6:11-14; 10:15; 11;10 and 13:2-5).

God called on Barak to destroy King Jabin's army and God promised him victory. However, Barak, an example of the weak men in those days, would not go unless Deborah went with him (Judges 3:7,8). Deborah warned that, if she went, he would forfeit to a woman the honor that should have been his (Judges 4:9). Just as she prophesied, his weakness resulted in shame. A woman killed the enemy king. Barak did diligently fight in the battle, and elsewhere in scripture Barak (sometimes called Bedan), not Deborah, is given credit for leading Israel to victory (1 Samuel 12:9-11; Hebrews 11:32). **Perhaps Deborah's greatest success was encouraging a God-appointed leader rather than trying to exalt herself.**

Isaiah describes in a negative light people who have children as oppressors and women as ruler (Isaiah 3:11,12). **God can and has blessed women-led ministries over men, but how much more would he bless if His pattern were followed more closely?**

Some churches misinterpret a support of male leadership as a suppression of women. This line of reasoning seems to stem more from the modern feminist and woman's liberation movements than from the Bible. In the long run everyone loses when the women take over.

History has shown that when women in the church start competing, men often leave. Lyle Schaller explains what has been happening in liberal churches where women have been assertive. **"In congregations with a long tradition of women being eligible for all lay-leadership offices, the male leadership has not only dropped out of leadership roles, but dropped out of active participation in the congregation."** [1]

When men hold the main leadership roles in the home or church, the women still have more left to do than they can possibly get done. Allowing the men to carry the overall leadership responsibility (1 Timothy 2:11-12; 1 Corinthians 14:35) frees the women to concentrate on those things they are designed to do best.

Conclusion

Women today continue to struggle to gain authority over men, to strive with man. Sometimes, like Eve, they get their way. The men, like Adam, passively relinquish their leadership. But such women, although they may in part enjoy the triumph, inwardly feel disgust for the men who gave them control. One bossy, domineering woman was overheard berating her husband, "Why can't you be a man?" She would have done well to ask herself, "How have I encouraged his leadership?"

"Going back to Adam and Eve, the natural sinful tendency of men is to be irresponsible, and for women to be dominant. When these two ancient male and female sin complexes are maximized, a society is in an accelerated decline... Previously... Women understood they were the power behind the throne, and that the hand which rocked the cradle ruled the world. Today, there is no one behind the throne in too many cases, or the throne is abandoned. And the hand that rocks the cradle is a day-care bureaucrat." [2]

Eve is remembered for leading her husband astray and destroying his leadership. In contrast the Titus 2 Model and the Proverbs 31 woman discovered the joy in helping the men in their lives develop their fullest potential. Personally they flourished under strong leadership. Godly women help build stronger male leaders. Everyone benefits from the results.

1 Schnaller, Lyle. "The Changing Focus of Church Finances," Leadership, Spring, 1981, p. 15. Used by permission.
2 McMaster, R.E., Jr. "Gentlemen," Chalcedon Report, June, 1990, p.3.

TRAINING OTHER WOMEN BY EXAMPLE

1. What type of women are to be exhorted by male leadership to teach or train other women (Titus 2:1-3)?

2. Titus 2:3-5 lists a catalogue of major training needs among women. Name at least one way you can encourage a friend to:

   love her husband

   love her children

   be pure

   be a home lover

   do good

   be obedient to her husband

3. What happens if women fail to teach these things (Titus 2:5)? Do you know a way this is happening today?

4. Compare 1 Corinthians 11:8-9 with Galatians 3:27-29. Explain the difference between the worth of a woman and her God-given role.

5. Consider the following New Testament writings, and explain God's plan for leadership in the church:

   1 Corinthians 14:34
   1 Timothy 2:8-14
   1 Timothy 3:1-7

6. Some women fight for their "rights" in leading men. In light of God's purposes, why do you think real inner contentment comes more from creatively complementing men than from competing with them?

God's Priceless Woman

74

© Wanda Kennedy Sanseri

TRAINING OTHER WOMEN BY EXAMPLE

"Teach the young women... that the word of God be not blasphemed"
(Titus 2:4-5).

Pat had no idea how much impact she had on the Christian woman. From Pat's perspective she only served simple meals in her home to a week-end guest. But the new believer, the daughter of an aggressive, domineering woman, had rarely seen a creative, happy homemaker. During the evening she watched Pat interface with her husband. She sensed love, harmony, fulfillment and peace.

The next day Pat invited this same guest to attend a "feminar," a workshop for women. At the activity several mature Christian women shared Scriptures such as Proverbs 31 and Titus 2. The new, radical ideas excited the imagination of the young believer. She linked the teaching at the seminar with the life model she saw in Pat. Without knowing it Pat fulfilled the injunction to train the younger women.

In modern times women like Pat are rare and valuable, a crown to their husbands (Proverbs 12:4), and a blessing to the community (Proverbs 31:20). Titus 2:3-5 outlines the profile of this kind of woman, listing the prerequisites for training others, highlighting key areas to teach and warning of the consequences if we fail to instruct the younger women.

The Prerequisites for Godly Teaching

The apostle lists specific qualifications for training others. Some of the conditions are common for both men and women.

1. SOUND DOCTRINE is the first requirement for discipling others (Titus 2:1). She should understand the gospel and the basics of the faith (Lessons 3-4). In other words she should fear the Lord. In German the phrase "sound doctrine" is translated, "healthy teaching." Doctrine is foundational to behavior.

2. THE TESTIMONY OF A GODLY LIFE is the second requirement. Those who train others should be sensible, worthy of respect, self-controlled, and sound in faith, in love and in endurance (Titus 2:2). The women in particular should display reverent behavior (Lessons 5,6), restrain from gossip (Lessons 7, 8), and avoid much wine (Lessons 9, 10). In summary they must be able to set a high standard and teach what is good (Titus 2:3).

The following are NOT prerequisites for teaching:

1. THE SPIRITUAL GIFT OF TEACHING IS NOT ESSENTIAL for those who train or encourage women. It is valuable to have a woman in the body who has the spiritual gift of organizing curriculum logically for teaching purposes. However, the teaching

ministry among women is not limited to those few supernaturally gifted to teach. The woman with the gift of helps can train wives to love their husbands; the saint with the gift of mercy can show the mothers how to love their children; the woman with the gift of faith can encourage the wives to obey their mates. A woman can work through any spiritual gift to edify other women in the specific areas described in Titus 2.

2. THE NATURAL INCLINATION TOWARD PUBLIC SPEAKING IS NOT NECESSARY. Edifying training is limited more by manner of life than by public speaking expertise. Although group teaching is important, to be life-changing the seminar times need to be supported by informal or one-on-one training situations. Other translations render the "teach" in Titus 2:4 as "train", "show", or "encourage". The picture is one of a sister demonstrating, challenging, explaining, directing and uplifting. The requirement in view here is "example teaching."

3. MARRIAGE IS NOT GIVEN AS A REQUIREMENT to teach women. God can and does give some single women insight to minister to wives and mothers. The Scriptures explain the reason this is possible. "One who is unmarried is concerned about the things of the Lord...but one who is married is concerned about the things of the world... how she may please her husband" (1 Corinthians 7:32-34, NASB). A married woman must put her family before her ministry to others. Only the single woman is free to dedicate herself wholeheartedly to others—whether it be other singles, children or married people.

Although the teacher does not have to be married herself, she does need to be well-versed in God's pattern for the successful home. If the instructor has never learned how to submit to male leadership in the church, she will not be able to teach women submission to their husbands. If she has not learned to understand the needs of children, she will not be able to teach mothers how to love their offspring. If she does not understand the problems of married life, she will not be able to prepare single women for their future roles.

The Major Teaching Topics for Women

The apostle admonishes the women to teach the young women in those vital areas affecting a woman's world—her home, her dress, her family, her ministry. If we fail, the Lord himself is dishonored (Titus 2:3-5). What is involved in helping in these areas? The following lessons will investigate each of these points in depth, but by way of introduction we will summarize the catalogue of things a godly woman needs to teach.

1. HOW DOES A WOMAN LOVE HER HUSBAND (Lessons 13,14)? She seeks to meet his needs. Such as:

a. **Completing** Him as His Helper Fit (Genesis 1:28; 2:18)
b. **Providing** Physical Satisfaction (1 Corinthians 7:3-5)
c. **Showing** Acceptance for Him as a Leader (Ephesians 5:22)
d. **Giving** Him Admiration (Ephesians 5:33)

2. HOW DOES A WOMAN LOVE HER CHILDREN (Lessons 15,16)? She assists her husband in training them for productive lives, building in them character and wisdom. Spiritual training involves several aspects:

a. **Teaching**	Structured and Informal (Deuteronomy 6:6-9)
b. **Disciplining**	Out of Love (Proverbs 13:24)
c. **Communicating**	Faith (1Timothy 1:5; Hebrews 11:23-39)

3. WHY SHOULD A WOMAN MODEL PURITY (Lessons 17,18)? A woman, as the "glory of man" (1 Corinthians 11:7), can influence a man's ability to worship. A woman can dress in an alluring way or sit carelessly, stirring a man's curiosity as to what else can be seen and thereby distracting him. The discreet woman, by reserving her sensual powers for the privacy of her marriage bed, can help men concentrate on the Lord so they can fulfill their role of praying publicly (1 Timothy 2:8-9).

4. WHAT IS INVOLVED IN KEEPING THE HOME (Lessons 19,20)?

a. **Organizing the Household.** Adapting to the likes of her husband, she prepares food, buys and maintains clothing, oversees cleaning, adds color, etc. (Proverbs 31).

b. **Providing Spirit of the Home.** She sets the atmosphere and makes the place a refuge filled with love, peace and security. Many women are successful organizers, providing clean homes and special meals, yet fail to create a pleasant atmosphere (Proverbs 15:17).

5. WHAT IS MEANT BY BEING GOOD (Lessons 21,22)? Good works are summarized in 1 Timothy 5:10. They involve caring for family needs as well as reaching out to others.

a. **Bringing up Children**
b. **Lodging Strangers**
c. **Ministering to Saints** (other Christians)
d. **Helping Afflicted**

6. WHY IS IT IMPORTANT TO SUBMIT TO HUSBANDS (Lessons 23,24)? A woman is not fulfilled when she rules over a weak husband, nor does she experience blessing when she constantly fights for control. A man is freer to show devotion and love to a woman who harmoniously works under his leadership.

Reasons for Supporting Male Leadership

Many women are not content to teach other women. They want to exert authority over men, to demonstrate their ability to achieve success in up front leadership. They fail to understand the big picture. The question in delegation of roles is not worth. In a football game the quarterback receives a lot of attention but he would never score touchdowns without a good support team. If all the players focused on learning skills in quarterbacking but no one learned to excel as blockers or linemen, the game would be lost.

1. SUPPLANTED MEN CREATE PROBLEMS. **Women can do many of the jobs done by men. They've proven that. But if women concentrate on leading men, what is left for men to do?** Some focus their energies on violence. Weldon Hardenbrook in <u>Missing From Action: Vanishing Manhood in America</u> reports that "Males account for 81 percent of arrests, 90 percent of those for violent crimes, 79 percent of those for property-crime offenses. Criminally irresponsible behavior in adults (as in juveniles) is an overwhelmingly male problem." [1]

2. MEN BIOLOGICALLY WERE DESIGNED TO LEAD. Paul Popenoe, the founder of the American Institute of Family Relations in Los Angeles who researched the biological differences between men and women, claims that man possesses on the average 50 percent more brute strength than a woman, and a significantly higher breathing power. Women have smaller lungs. Woman's blood contains more water and 20 percent fewer red cells. Since the red cells supply oxygen to the body cells, the woman tires more easily and is more prone to faint. Women outlive men by three to four years but their constitutional vitality is limited to life span. [2]

God made men with broad shoulders, strong muscles, and a large stature. He gave him a need to provide for and protect others, to give "honor unto the wife, as unto the weaker vessel" (1 Peter 3:7). When that need is taken away he feels useless and unmotivated.

3. WOMEN EXPERIENCE MIXED BLESSINGS WHEN THEY PREDOMINATE. **The fight to win prominence over men does not produce lasting satisfaction.** Unfortunately the women exalted by our society are often those who win promising career positions over men. A recent newspaper article featured ten leading women executives in San Francisco. They had made it to the top professionally, but without exception they were all newly divorced. They sacrificed their marriages for their careers. What a price to pay for "success".

Annie Gottlieb described the disappointment of the women's liberation movement in the October, 1983 issue of <u>Mc Call's</u>.

> Have you noticed? Men and women aren't as different as they used to be. Women now don surgeons' gowns and astronauts' space suits. Men are more nurturing to children and are accepting more responsibility for the household.
> The majority of women seem to like the prospect of a unisex world—except for one nagging problem: **many of today's men, mysteriously, lack a special vibrancy, vitality, gusto, pride that we once recognized as distinctively masculine.** "Much is being said among American women today about the death of vital men,"

Betty Friedan wrote recently. "I go into a town to lecture, and I hear about all the wonderful, dynamic women who have emerged in every field in that town. But frequently, whatever the age of the woman, she says, **"The men seem so dull and gray now. They're dreary, they're flat."**

4. SOCIETY BENEFITS WHEN MEN LEAD WISELY. When women learn the art of building men, everyone benefits. Male aggressive tendencies are tamed, passive men are revitalized, timid men are strengthened. Women gain satisfaction from supporting successful leaders. George Gilder in his thought-provoking book, <u>Men and Marriage</u>, explains,

"Women transform male lust into love; channel male wanderlust into jobs, homes and families; link man to specific children; rear children into citizens; change hunters into fathers; divert male will to power into a drive to create..." [3]

Women have the function which he describes as taming the barbarian in man. **"Women domesticate and civilize male nature. They can jeopardize male discipline and identity, and civilization as well, by merely giving up the role."** [4]

5. GOD INTENDED FOR WOMEN TO PROMOTE MALE LEADERSHIP. God intended for His creation order to prevail for the good of all. In the New Testament Paul writes, "I want you to understand that Christ is the head of every man, and the man is the head of a woman. . . . For man does not originate from woman, but woman from man; for indeed man was not created for woman's sake but woman for the man's sake" (1 Corinthians 11:3,8,9, NASB).

Role distinction is not a value judgment. Godly women are priceless in value. Men and women share equal significance, but different functions, different purposes. God made woman as man's completion, one who could encourage and assist him in developing his leadership potential. He designed her to be a special blessing to him, not his competitor.

Summary

All Christian women should strive to be "teachers of good things" as we share recipes, shop for dress patterns or just visit over a cup of tea. We should constantly evaluate our personal walk, asking ourselves: "Does my life inspire purity, self-control and seriousness of purpose? Do I guide other women to be better homemakers, wives and mothers? Does my spirit of contentment encourage them in their role? Are men stronger leaders to the glory of God because of me? Am I a teacher of good things?"

1 Hardenbrook, Weldon. <u>Missing from Action: Vanishing Manhood in America.</u> (Thomas Nelson Publishers: Nashville, Tenn.),1987, p. 109.

2 Smalley, Gary. <u>The Joy of Committed Love.</u> (Zondervan: Grand Rapids, Michigan) p. 15.

3 Gilder, George. <u>Men and Marriage</u>. (Pelican Publishing Company: Gretna, Louisiana, 1987), p. 5.

4 Ibid., p.12.

MARY: A WOMAN WHO LOVED HER HUSBAND

1. Read Luke 1:26-56. What was God's evaluation of Mary? Some claim she was sinless. What phrase indicates Mary recognized her own sinfulness (v.47)?

2. How does obedience to the first command in Matthew 22:37 relate to the second? (See 1 John 4:19-21)

3. Compare Mary's and Hannah's prayers (Luke 1:46-55; 1 Samuel 2:1-10). Notice characteristics of God referred to by both.

   Luke 1:46   1 Samuel 2:2
   Luke 1:49   1 Samuel 2:3
   Luke 1:51   1 Samuel 2:7
   Luke 1:52   1 Samuel 2:5
   Luke 1:54,55   1 Samuel 2:10

   Contrast Hannah's relationship with her husband before and after she reconciled with God (1 Samuel 1:7-8 ; 18-19). What type of relationship do you believe Mary had with Joseph?

4. What do we know of Mary's moral character (Luke 1:27ff)? Why is fidelity an important part of love in marriage (Proverbs 6:32-35)?

   Faithfulness to a mate is one aspect of purity. What other responsibility does a woman have (1 Corinthians 7:5)?

   Joseph and Mary mutually abstained from marital intimacy (Matt 1:25). How do we know they did not continue to abstain (Matt 13:55,56)?

5. A loving wife shares her husband's goals. List ways we see Mary and Joseph united (Matthew 2:13-14; Luke 2:22, 41; Luke 2:42-48).

6. Evaluate your own life. How do you need to strengthen your love for God? Name one specific thing you can do for Him this week. If you are married how can you strengthen love for your husband?

MARY: A WOMAN WHO LOVED HER HUSBAND

*"Teach the young women . . . to love their husbands. . .
that the word of God be not blasphemed"*
(Titus 2:4-5).

"Hail thou that art highly favored," the angel greeted Mary of Nazareth." Thou hast found favor with God" (Luke 1:28). Mary was honored when God selected her to mother Jesus. Why was she blessed from among women?

Some have gone so far as to claim that Mary had a sinless nature. Such a view cannot be supported by Scripture. All descendants of Adam inherit a sin nature (Romans 3:23), a fact Mary recognized when she acknowledged her need for a savior (Luke 1:47). Like all Jewish women, she went to the temple for purification after childbirth (Luke 2:22). She sacrificed either two turtledoves or two pigeons, one for a burnt offering and one for a sin offering. Rather than honored for a sinless nature, Mary was honored for a humble awareness of her need for God and her wholehearted surrender to Him. She understood that salvation is available only through faith in the Messiah, not based on her own merit (Acts 4:12).

Mary Loved God First

Mary demonstrates love, first for God and then for her husband and others (Matthew 22:37). How do we see her love in action?

1. MARY GAVE OF HERSELF SACRIFICIALLY. An angel appeared to Mary and told her she would bear a son. Mary questioned how. She did not protest the ramifications a virgin pregnancy could produce. (Who would believe a pregnant, unwed mother was a virgin)? She questioned technicalities. The angel explained supernatural impregnation (Luke 1:34) and reminded her of God's miraculous power. Even Elizabeth, old and barren, had conceived, "for with God nothing shall be impossible" (Luke 1:35).

Mary could have been caught up with vital questions like: "Will Joseph believe I've been unfaithful?" or "Will I be unjustly stoned for immorality?" In Israel adultery was a capital offense (Deuteronomy 22:20-21). She was willing to submit herself to God's purposes no matter what the cost. She trusted God to solve the problem of her reputation. Mary answered the angel, "I am the Lord's servant. May it be to me as you have said" (Luke 1:38).

2. MARY KNEW GOD DEEPLY. Real love is based on knowledge. Mary spent in-depth time studying the Word of God. She knew the Psalms well and quoted them in her spontaneous prayer recorded in Luke 1:46-55. (Psalm 35:9; 103:17; 98:1 and 107:9).

She also knew about Hannah's prayer in 2 Samuel. Commentators feel it is more than coincidence that Mary's Magnificat so closely parallels Hannah's prayer of exaltation. Point by point, in an almost identical outline, Mary spontaneously paraphrased Hannah's prayer of praise recorded in Scripture hundreds of years earlier.

Mary and Hannah rejoiced over the Lord and salvation through Him (Luke 1:46-47;1 Samuel 2:1). They praised God for His **holiness** (Luke 1:49; 1 Samuel 2:2) and recognized His fair **justice** based on infinite **knowledge**. "He scatters the proud in the imagination of their heart." There is no place for false boasting before the One by whom all actions are weighed (Luke 1:51; 1 Samuel 2:3). They acknowledged His **sovereign control** by referring to His **power** to bring low and lift up and His ability to "put down the mighty" (Luke 1:52; 1 Samuel 2:4). Mary and Hannah both marveled at how God fills the hungry with good things and sends away the rich empty-handed (Luke 1:53; 1 Samuel 2:5). His method of operation is directly opposite to the world's system. Mary proclaimed with Hannah the **faithfulness** of God. He will fulfill the promise to exalt His anointed through the seed of Abraham (Luke 1:54-55; 1 Samuel 2:10).

Mary applied the Word to her life. She recognized God as holy, just, sovereign, faithful, merciful, strong and loving. Familiar with the promise made to Abraham, Mary realized that God planned to use her to fulfill prophecy (Luke 1:51-55). The long awaited Messiah was at hand. The angel had predicted that the child she was carrying would "reign over the house of Jacob forever; and of his kingdom there shall be no end" (Luke 1:33). Through faith in this promise, Mary did not need to fear being stoned in Israel. Nor did she need to fear her own eternal future. God was not only sending her a Savior, but He was also giving her the joy of being intimately involved with the fulfillment of his plan.

Mary Extended Her Love for God to Others

A proper love for God produces a proper love for people. "If anyone says, 'I love God,' yet hates his brother, he is a liar. For anyone who does not love his brother, whom he has seen, cannot love God, whom he has not seen. And he has given us this command: whoever loves God must also love his brother "(1 John 4:19-21). In a marriage between two Christians, the husband is also the brother in Christ to the wife.

In an earlier lesson we saw an example of how our relationship with God affects our relationship to our mate. Hannah suffered depression and her husband felt distressed by her gloom (1 Samuel 1:8-10). He loved her and felt helpless. A happy wife is a crown to her husband, but a sad wife is a public rebuke. When Hannah overcame her spiritual struggle, their marriage relationship drastically changed. They worshiped the Lord together (v.19) and she sang out with joy (2 Samuel 2:1).

Before Mary and Joseph married, they had individually established a solid relationship with God. We've compared Mary's and Hannah's prayers of praise. After Hannah's prayer her relationship with her husband improved. We can assume Mary and Joseph enjoyed a mutually rich relationship. Nothing indicates otherwise.

Mary modeled a number of characteristics of love. We will review a few.

1. A LOVING WIFE IS SPIRIT LED. Personal times with God flow over into our family and others. So it must have been with Mary and her deep devotional life. **Ephesians 5 records guidelines for husbands and wives. Before listing specific instructions for mates, Paul exhorts everyone to "be filled with the Spirit;** speaking to yourselves in psalms and hymns and spiritual songs, singing and making melody in your heart to the Lord" (Ephesians 5:18-21).

We should not confuse this natural sharing with preaching or nagging. A loving wife is growing in her personal life and is an encouragement for others spiritually. She prays diligently for her mate. While she does not depend on her husband's walk with God, she encourages his spiritual leadership.

One friend we'll call Jane shared with me a deep concern for her husband whom we will call Bob. He led the family in changing churches, but Jane perceived some serious doctrinal errors in the new church. She became frightened as she saw her husband swayed by the wrong teaching. Her first response to this distress was anger and tears. Bob became more stubborn. He focused on the good he saw and ignored glaring problems. She stayed home from church while he went alone, but she felt miserable that they were separated. She tried joining him and felt equally frustrated. Finally she came to us in distress. Together we prayed for them, not only for the husband's eyes to be opened, but also for grace for the wife.

Four agonizing weeks passed, but she learned to step back and let the Lord direct her mate. A happy couple invited us over for dinner to relay the positive ending to this story. One of the leaders in the questionable church started an argument with my friend's husband and told him he did not belong in their church. Bob told us that then he saw potential dangers from which he had to protect his family. God answered the wife's prayers and arranged circumstances so the husband could see for himself the need to lead the family away from an unhealthy situation.

2. A LOVING WIFE IS PURE. Mary remained a virgin as a single woman (Luke 1:27ff). Because of their unusual situation, Mary and Joseph abstained from normal marital intimacy until after the birth of Jesus (Matthew 1:25). Some traditions claim Mary maintained her virginity throughout life. We know she did not. She mothered other children: James, Joseph, Simeon, Judas and daughters (Matthew 13:55,56).

God warns couples not to deprive each other of marital love except for mutual consent and that for a limited time for prayer. "Then come together again so that Satan will not tempt you because of your lack of self-control" (1 Corinthians 7:5). Sex was designed for marriage and is not wrong when used as God intended. A woman shows love to her husband by regularly responding to him physically. A man needs a woman who lavishes him with her love, meeting his physical needs. Yet he simultaneously needs the assurance of her fidelity to him. Proverbs 6:30-35 describes a man's fury at discovering another man with his wife. He may be able to forgive a thief who steals all his possessions, but he will not accept compensation when a man steals his wife.

3. A LOVING WIFE IS NOT SELF-SEEKING. Mary modeled a meek and quiet spirit. She recognized herself as a "handmaid of the Lord." Instead of feeling like she deserved the honor God bestowed on her, she saw Him operating out of mercy to exalt one of low degree. We can assume her humble spirit helped her love and support her husband.

4. A LOVING WIFE SHARES HER HUSBAND'S GODLY GOALS. Joseph and Mary functioned as a team. They jointly shared hardships like the flight into Egypt (Matthew 2:13,14). For a time they gave up home and family to protect the Christ child. They regularly worshipped together (Luke 2:22,41). The pair searched for twelve-year-old Jesus when they thought that he was lost (Luke 2:42-48).

Conclusion

Mary teaches us that love is a commitment that requires sacrificial action. Deep, mature love for our husbands springs from a deep devotion to God.

ENCOURAGING LOVE FOR HUSBANDS

1. Read Ephesians 5:22,33. Name two positive actions a loving wife needs to display. Explain why these are important.

   Define reverence.

2. Contrast reverence with nagging or belittling.

   Describe a time when either you or a woman you know either reverenced or nagged her husband. What was the result?

3. Read Romans 12:9-12. List specific ways to love others, particularly your mate.

4. Read 1 Corinthians 13. List characteristics of love.

   Select two characteristics you need to strengthen in your relationship to someone close to you.

5. In your own words define "love".

   Why does God consider love to be vital in the life of a believer? (Colossians 3:12-14; 1 Corinthians 13:8).

6. Love "believes all things" (1 Corinthians 13:7). Name one area in which you can envision future potential and growth in your leader. How will you help encourage him as he grows?

ENCOURAGING LOVE FOR HUSBANDS

"Her husband. . . praises her; many daughters
have done virtuously, but thou excellest them all."
(Proverbs 31: 28b-29)

How can a woman love her husband? Some women may respond, "How can I love him the way he treats me? He forgets my birthday, never helps with the children, thinks only of himself. How does God expect me to respond affectionately to one who neglects me?"

One actress confided, "Marriage is wonderful. It's my husband I can't stand." She missed the point. Love is not an emotion, a quiver in the liver, a gushy response to amorous treatment.

The love modeled by Jesus Christ is an initiating love. "We love because he first loved us." (1 John 4:19). We can choose to love as an act of the will. If a woman is married, God intends for her to remain with her husband and not look around for a more desirable partner. He understands the pain of rejection she may sometimes experience. "Under three things the earth trembles" and one of these is " an unloved woman who is married" (Proverbs 30:21,23).

Retaliation or withdrawal will not satisfactorily correct the unloved feeling. A woman can often help revitalize her marriage if she determines, with God's grace, to love her husband unconditionally. Lost love can be regained.

Ella May Miller relays the experience of one wife:

> My marriage was about to break up. I didn't love John, but one day I let Jesus take over my life. I began to ask, "How would I act if I did love my husband?" Then I consciously began learning his likes and dislikes. I prepared his favorite dishes. I joined his hobbies. I bought surprises to put in his lunch at noon. Now I love him with all my heart. But the greatest reward came the other day when our teenager said, "Mom, I'm lucky." "Oh," I answered. "Why?" "You and Dad love each other. You'd be surprised how many kids have parents who fight and quarrel most of the time." [1]

Love for Husband a Number One Priority

Martin Luther once said, "Some marriages were motivated by mere lust, but mere lust is felt even by fleas and lice. Love begins when we wish to serve others."[2] As

---

Christian women we are responsible to love our neighbors. Since our husband is our closest neighbor, he should receive the deepest share of our love and respect.

Proverbs 31 and Titus 2 can be divided into basic relationships in a woman's life. The husband is placed first in both passages before children, homemaking responsibilities or benevolence. **The husband and wife relationship is of primary importance because all other functions hinge on the strength of the marriage.** The priority of the husband is no less significant in second marriages. Children from a previous marriage may predate the new marriage, but must not distract from the significance of the new marriage vows. Parents train children to leave home some day.

The bond of matrimony is designed by God to be permanent. Women who emotionally place their children over their mates make poor mother-in-laws because they will be competitive with the their daughter-in-laws rather than supportive.

Actions of Love from Ephesians 5

Women are exhorted to support their husbands in two ways in Ephesians 5. We are to accept their leadership. Submission as to the Lord will be discussed in Lessons 23 and 24. The wife is also challenged to reverence her husband (v.33).

The Scripture does not just challenge wives to reverence husbands, but it commands respect for all authority figures. We are to honor the king or the government officials, (1 Peter 2:13-17), esteem spiritual leaders highly for their work's sake (1 Thessalonians 5:12-13) and honor parents (Ephesians 6:1-2) and employers (1 Timothy 6:1). The single woman can model reverence for her leaders and thereby encourage married women to love their husbands.

The purpose for reverencing one's leader is evident when we analyze the implications of not reverencing him. To reverence implies he is worthy of admiration, but nagging or belittling implies he is inadequate and unworthy of praise. Reverence helps build the leader's confidence. Nagging and belittling destroys confidence, stunts leadership development and tears down the sense of personal worth. **We can enlarge a leader through reverence.**

A woman can either destroy a man or help make him a bigger and better man. It would be simple to reverence a perfect leader, but few women learn the womanly art of building men. Honoring a fallible human is difficult. In fact, true reverence is only possible supernaturally. Yet God commands that we reverence those He has placed over us, and He also gives us the power to obey His commands. A wise woman realizes that she can help strengthen a leader more by giving him honest praise than by finding fault in him. So she will ask God to help change her thoughts from criticism to love. As she turns her attention from negative traits to positive characteristics, her admiration for her leader will naturally grow.

Reverence means "notice, prefer, love and respect." It can be defined most fully by considering synonyms and antonyms. If one does not reverence a leader, she will either nag or belittle him.

Consider an amplification of these terms:

REVERENCE	NAG / BELITTLE
show respect	*find fault*
honor	*scold*
defer to	*pester*
regard	*vex*
praise	*urge*
venerate	*make small*
esteem	*make less important*
admire	*make seem little*

Actions of Love from Romans 12:9-12

The letter to the Romans lists characteristics of love. We will investigate a few not covered elsewhere.

1. SINCERITY. "Love must be sincere" (v.9). A love relationship needs to be based on truth. Love is trustworthy, reliable, dependable. Truth is not a license to be unkind. Love does not speak thoughtlessly. It protects the loved one. But it does not deceive.

2. COMMITMENT. "Be devoted to one another" (v.10). A movie star flippantly stated, "Marriage is a perfectly fine way to keep busy until the right man comes along." God intends marriage to be permanent. The marriage bond is not a provisional arrangement until you find someone better. A wife needs to be committed totally to her mate. Love is loyal.

3. FAITHFULNESS IN PRAYER (v.12). Our imperfect husbands need our prayer support. We need to pray for their growth, wise leadership, their purity, their deepest needs. Prayer is one of the greatest gifts of love we can give another.

Actions of Love from 1 Corinthians 13

Perfect love is described in 1 Corinthians 13, the love chapter of Scripture. We do well to measure ourself against these perfect standards:

1. PATIENCE. Love is long-suffering, concerned for the other. We need to ask ourselves, "Am I easily offended? Can I endure injury? Am I easily excitable over decisions my husband makes? Do I have a tendency to take matters into my own hands? Do I give my husband room to fail?"

2. KINDNESS. Love gives for the good of others. This form of kindness is a deed or action, not just nice attitudes or a sweet spirit. The Greek root word for kindness is "useful." We should ask ourselves, "Do I work for my mate's welfare? What can I do for my husband that would be useful, meaningful or helpful?"

3. JOY OVER SUCCESS OF ANOTHER. In honor give preference to one another (Romans 12:10). Ask: "Do I begrudge my husband of his job, friends, ministry, or opportunities? Am I excited about working for the success of my husband even if it works against my own?" Love is not jealous or envious. "But if you have bitter envy and self-seeking in your hearts, do not boast and lie against the truth. This wisdom does not descend from above, but is earthly, sensual, demonic. For where envy and self-seeking exist, confusion and every evil thing will be there" (James 3:14-16, NKJV).

4. HUMILITY. Non-intimidating love does not exalt itself over another. It is not arrogant or puffed up. Pride only breeds quarrels (Proverbs 13:10). The Lord resists the haughty. "Pride and arrogance and the evil way and the perverse mouth I hate." (Proverbs 8:13, NKJV). We can ask ourselves, "Do I brag in an effort to make him feel inferior? Do I flaunt myself and my achievements or needs. Do I correct him in public?"

5. CONSIDERATION, THOUGHTFULNESS. Love does not act unbecomingly. We can ask ourselves, "Do I treat my mate courteously? Do I care about his feelings? Or am I rude, impolite, inconsiderate or indifferent? Do I have a grateful spirit or does my husband feel he is a prisoner of my expectations?"

6. UNSELFISHNESS. Love does not seek its own. Love does not focus on rights. Love concentrates on the needs of the partner. We might ask: "Am I willing to provide for his physical needs even when I'm tired? Can he trust me to budget for household expenses wisely? Do I think of his plans when I schedule events? Do I give him adequate quiet time for personal prayer and study? Do I consume him for myself or do I think of his needs over my own?"

7. ABILITY TO OVERLOOK OFFENSES AND FORGIVE. Love is not easily provoked and does not retaliate when wronged. Love overlooks an offense, endures hurt and forgives. It keeps no records of wrongs. Love assumes the best. We might ask ourselves: "Do I squelch others by focusing on their faults, or do I enlarge them by

looking for strengths to compliment? Do I give them the benefit of the doubt when I misunderstand an action?"

8. VISION FOR GROWTH. "Let love be without hypocrisy. Abhor what is evil. Cling to what is good" (Romans 12:9, NKJV). Love does not tolerate or encourage wrong doing. It does not delight in what offends God or hurts people. Love rejoices in godliness and truth. It thinks no evil. We might ask ourselves, "Do I think well of my mate? Can I see past the hurts to the potential for the future?"

"Love suffers long [shows patience] and is kind; love does not envy [overcomes jealousy of the success of others]; love does not parade itself, is not puffed up [displays humility]; does not behave rudely [shows politeness and consideration], does not seek its own [is unselfish], is not provoked, thinks no evil; does not rejoice in iniquity, but rejoices in the truth [demonstrates understanding and forgiveness]; bears all things believes all things, hopes all things, endures all things. Love never fails . . . . And now abide faith, hope, love, these three; but the greatest of these is love" (1 Corinthians 13:7,8,13 NKJV).

A man's greatest need is respect. We best show love when we demonstrate esteem for the number one man in our life (our father or husband). We need to learn to reverence our leaders and to encourage others to do likewise. Women often get together and go on and on about the failures of the men in their lives. It takes just one person to change the direction of the conversation to one of appreciation.

"As the elect of God, holy and beloved, put on tender mercies, kindness, humbleness of mind, meekness, longsuffering: bearing with one another, and forgiving one another, if anyone has a complaint against another; even as Christ forgave you, so you also must do. But above all these things put on love, which is the bond of perfection" (Colossians 3:12-14 NKJV).

---

1 Ella Mae Miller. <u>A Woman in Her Home.</u> Chicago, IL: Moody Press, 1968, p.20.

2 Petersen, William. <u>Martin Luther Had a Wife</u>. Wheaton, IL: Tyndale, 1983, p.35.

STUDY GUIDE   LESSON 15

JOCHEBED: A WOMAN WHO LOVED CHILDREN

1. Amram and Jochebed were the only parents recorded in Scripture to have three children all in leadership in Israel (Micah 6:4). In what ways did Moses pattern his life after his parents' early training (Hebrews 11:23,27)?

   How was his thinking different from the world's (Hebrews 11:24-28)?

2. Describe the spiritual conditions in the nation of Israel at the time of Moses (Joshua 24:14; Ezekiel 20:6-8). How can we teach children to be in the world but not of the world?

3. Paraphrase Psalm 144:11-12.

4. Our training goals and activities should be complementary. Can you think of common teaching sources for children (i.e., books, games, toys, traditions, etc.) that should be avoided? Why?

   Can you think of sources that should be encouraged? Explain.

5. God inspired Moses, the recipient of early training, to record guidelines for training children. List some of the techniques referred to in Deuteronomy 6:4-9).

6. Name one child or mother you can prayerfully encourage this week. What will you do specifically to encourage this person?

JOCHEBED: A WOMAN WHO LOVED CHILDREN

"Her children arise up and call her blessed"
(Proverbs 31:28)

One couple in Scripture, Amram and Jochebed, is remembered not only for their own walk of faith, but for the walk of faith of their three children. No other Israelite family ever brought forth three great leaders (Micah 6:4). Moses became a prophet, Aaron a high priest (Exodus 28:1), and Miriam a prophetess (Exodus 15:20).

This family, like modern day parents, lived in a time period of spiritual decay and idolatry. Even the children of Israel followed the rites of the pagan Egyptians (Joshua 24:14). Ezekiel summarized the judgment of God on the people for their rebellion against Him at this time (Ezekiel 20:6-8).

In this setting Jochebed mothered three godly children, the greatest being the leader Moses. The most noteworthy characteristic of this family's training is the way they modeled trust in God. Hebrews 11:23 states that they were "not afraid of the king's commandment." They risked their lives in an effort to save their son from the threat of death. Pharaoh decreed that all male Hebrew babies be thrown into the Nile. These parents, while creatively obeying the order, still protected their infant offspring. They lovingly placed him in a floating basket and put it among the reeds and committed him to God's care. Thus, helpless Moses was rescued from his watery grave. The Egyptian princess recovered Moses from the Nile, and not knowing that Jochebed was his mother, appointed her as his wet nurse, thereby paying the natural parents to be "foster" parents for her adopted son.

As a child Moses probably heard often how his name, which means "to draw out," could be traced back to his deliverance from the waters. He grew up witnessing in his parents a dynamic walk of faith. Their testimony helped reproduce in him a trust in God . In the New Testament chapter listing giants of the faith Moses, too, was described as one "not fearing the wrath of the king" (Hebrews 11:27).

In time he moved to the palace, but not before he received godly training. How did he respond to the potential of power and influence in Egypt?

"By faith Moses, when he was come to years, refused to be called the son of Pharaoh's daughter; Choosing rather to suffer affliction with the people of God, than to enjoy the pleasures of sin for a season; Esteeming the reproach of Christ greater riches than the treasures in Egypt: for he had respect unto the recompense of the reward. By faith he forsook Egypt, not fearing the wrath of the king: for he endured, as seeing him who is invisible."
(Hebrews 11:24-28).

The training of Moses' early days prepared him to give up reign over the greatest nation on earth. Amram and Jochebed inspired him to stand alone in an alien environment. His greatest aspirations were not worldly success but eternal riches. Through the pen of Moses God inspired guidelines for future parents.

Guidelines for Trainers of Children

The process of nurturing a child demands concerted effort and hard work. But "a child left to himself bringeth his mother to shame . . . . Correct thy son, and he will give thee rest; yea, he shall give delight unto thy soul" (Proverbs 29:15b,17). God inspired Moses, the recipient of early godly training, to record in Deuteronomy 6:4-9 some secrets of guiding young ones. We will consider four aspects of training which Moses emphasizes.

1. TRAINERS SHOULD BE SPIRITUALLY MATURE. First, the teacher must be spiritually growing. "The LORD our God, the LORD is one," exclaimed Moses. "Love the LORD your God with all your heart, with all your soul, and with all your might. And these words which I command you today shall be in your heart; you shall teach them diligently to your children" (Deuteronomy 6:4-7, NKJV).

The effective leader of children needs a dynamic, vibrant walk with God. "But the mercy of the Lord is from everlasting to everlasting upon those who fear him, and his righteousness unto children's children" (Psalm 103:17). "Only take heed to thyself, and keep thy soul diligently, lest thou forget the things which thine eyes have seen, and lest they depart from thy heart all the days of thy life; but teach them to thy sons, and thy sons' sons "(Deuteronomy 4:9).

Training involves transmitting one's life pattern to others. The effect that a parent's relationship to God has on future generations is demonstrated vividly by analyzing two family histories.

The Max Jukes family demonstrates the Scriptural principle that the sins of the parents will be inflicted on the second and third generation. Five hundred and forty descendants of this atheistic household were traced revealing the following results: 310 of them died as paupers, 150 were criminals, 7 were murderers, 100 were drunkards and more than half of the women were prostitutes. His descendants cost the state one and one-fourth million dollars.

In contrast, 1,394 descendants of Jonathan and Sarah Edwards, God-fearing contemporaries of Max Jukes, were traced. Their lineage held large numbers of preachers, missionaries, college presidents, professors, judges, lawyers, doctors, army and navy officers, prominent authors, and public officials including senators, several governors and one vice-president of the United States. Their descendants did not cost the state anything. [1]

Those who serve the Lord can prayerfully claim the promise given to Jacob, "I will pour my Spirit upon thy seed, and my blessing upon thine offspring; and they shall spring up as among grass, like willows by the water courses" (Isaiah 44:3b-4).

2. LEADERS NEED TO GIVE FORMAL INSTRUCTION IN THE SCRIPTURES. Moses reminded us that we can only teach what we believe ourselves. He goes on to demonstrate the importance of a plan for action. The imparting of learned truths must be done systematically. Moses continued, "thou shalt teach them diligently unto thy children" (Deuteronomy 6:7b). Occasional or erratic devotional periods are not synonymous with diligent training. The ideal program is conducted regularly. Scripture memory and regular Bible study are important. My husband has taken our boys through The Shorter Catachism by G.I. Williamson. When our sons became old enough to read we assigned them one morning a week to share a passage of Scripture from their own private devotions.

3. TEACHERS SHOULD REINFORCE SCRIPTURE IN EVERYDAY LIFE. Although the formal training is vital, its value is limited without reinforcement in informal periods of the day. Moses adds to teaching diligently the injunction, "and shalt talk of them when thou liest down, and when thou risest up" (v.7). That means that we teach during every waking moment: at home, away from home, from the rising in the morning to the retiring at night. Everything we do must consistently communicate the same concept. All activities and events should focus on the same general aims. Repetition and variety are required training techniques. Since a child's life is filled with hours of play, it is important to use play as a training tool.

a. Children's Music and Books. Much of a child's conception of life is formulated through books and music. To the younger child pictures are as significant as the actual words. Evaluate all material carefully. Sometimes simple alterations can be made. An excellent book about daddies had one problem. The father often smoked a pipe, giving the impression that smoking was mature and manly. I used white opaque correction fluid to blot out all traces of pipes. Underlying themes should be considered as well as modeling effects. Use Biblical standards to measure contemporary sources. Does the story erroneously teach that the end justifies the means? Does the story minimize or glamorize the power of evil?

Books Children Love: A Guide to the Best Children's Literature by Elizabeth Wilson lists good quality books for children written from a Judeo-Christian perspective.

b. Family Traditions. It is good to have traditions. We need them for security and social fellowship. However, specific traditions are not necessarily good in themselves. In fact many are harmful. We must learn to evaluate the training effect. If the tradition communicates a non-acceptable philosophy, do not maintain it for sentimental reasons. Throw it out and feel the freedom to develop new traditions that are biblically sound and personally edifying. Traditions should not distract from Jesus but rather enhance His message.

1. Halloween, known at our house as "Jesus is Lord's Day," can provide a challenging opportunity for witnessing. Everyone in the family can bag goodies and staple tracts on the outside (geared primarily for parents). Small children can be told that people may come to the door dressed in strange, or perhaps sad costumes. The children can help share about Jesus and learn to give instead of bribe. (*Trick-or-treat* is a threat which implies people owe them something and revenge is acceptable.) Rather than being caught up in Satan's realm of witches and goblins, Jesus Christ is given the preeminent place. In our home our children knock on our bedroom door and announce, "Jesus is Lord!" We give them a treat and suggest they tell a friend. If they return with a brother or playmate and repeat the "special" words, they are rewarded again.

More recently we have discovered an even better alternative. On October 31, 1517, Martin Luther nailed the 95 theses on the door of Christ Church in Wittenburg, Germany. We commemorate this event that changed the world. For Reformation Day each year we study a different reformer and play games like "pin the theses to the door."

2. Christmas and Easter are excellent teaching opportunities. However, Satan has a clever way of numbing the effect of our religious holidays. Instead of squelching the observance, he presents detractors. For Christmas the attraction is Santa Claus. For Easter it is the Easter Bunny. Like Santa, the Easter Bunny is given divine attributes as he miraculously leaves baskets of goodies in countless homes on the night before Easter. An incident observed several years ago demonstrates the effect of the Easter Bunny story on a group of children all from Christian homes. Two grade school boys asked their eight-year old cousin, "The Easter Bunny is going to bring us big chocolate eggs tomorrow. What are you going to get?" In all seriousness the younger cousin said, "Oh, I hope I get chocolate eggs!" He knelt down and earnestly prayed, "Dear Easter Bunny, please bring me chocolate eggs, too! Thank you. Amen."

Just as the miracle of the virgin birth is minimized through simultaneously teaching that the myth of Santa is true, so the miracle of the resurrection is diminished because of the Easter Bunny myth. Rabbits do not lay eggs. But eggs do have religious significance. The Easter egg has been, since 1500 years before the Christian era, a scared emblem of pagan worship. "The Hindu fables celebrate their mundane egg as of a golden color. The people of Japan make their sacred egg to have been brazen. In China, at this hour, dyed or painted eggs are used in sacred festivals, even as in this country."[2]

Many are afraid that if they are distinctly Christian in their celebrations that the children will miss some fun. However, many families find the opposite to be the case. When the joy is centered on a make-believe story the excitement is lost once the child discovers the "secret." When the creative activity is built around the person of Jesus, the joy intensifies every year. Young and old are enriched. Gary and I have written an age integrated devotional guide for Christmas called, Advent Foretold.

4. LEADERS WOULD DO WELL TO VISUALLY DISPLAY BIBLICAL TRUTHS. In addition to maintaining personal spiritual vitality, and training children both formally and informally, leaders should use pictorial illustrations to reinforce truths. Moses suggested finally for us to, "Tie them as symbols on your hands (your actions) and bind them on your forehead (your thoughts). Write them on the door frames of your house

(when entering home) and your gates (when leaving home)" (Deuteronomy 6:8-9 NIV). Key Bible passages or inspirational thoughts displayed in the home can have a profound effect for good.

5. LEADERS DO WELL TO CORRECT NEGATIVE BEHAVIOR. God gives parents the responsibility to help build in their child a fear of the Lord. We do this through our own example (John 13:15; 1 Corinthians 11:1) and from positive instruction (Psalm 32:8).

Reward positive behavior and correct negative behavior. Punishment should never be administered to "get back" at a child. Godly training focuses on the child's needs to develop self-control. The benefit of punishment is determined by what the act of discipline communicates. Ignoring may imply rejection. Scolding may imply lack of acceptance. Spanking can imply either loving guidance or bullying, depending on the manner in which it is executed.

a. Prerequisites for Effective Discipline
Soft voice -- "A soft answer turns away wrath, but a harsh word stirs up anger" (Proverbs 15:1 NKJV).
Calm spirit -- "An angry man stirs up strife, and a furious man abounds in transgression" (Proverbs 29:22 NKJV).
Enough love to be willing to bother -- "As many as I love, I rebuke and chasten" (Revelations 3:19).
Controlled manner -- He that is quick-tempered acts foolishly. (Proverbs 14:17) "He who is slow to wrath has great understanding, but he who is impulsive exalts folly. (Proverbs 14:29).
Consistency -- "Fathers, provoke not your children to anger, lest they be discouraged" (Colossians 3:21).

b. Benefits of Spanking as a Discipline
Shows Love -- "He who spares his rod hates his son, but he who loves him disciplines him promptly" (Proverbs 13:24 NKJV).
Demonstrates concern for long term benefits -- "Chasten your son while there is hope, and do not set your heart on his destruction" (Proverbs 19:18 NKJV).
Cleanses -- "Blows that hurt cleanse away evil, as do stripes the inner depts of the heart" (Proverbs 20:30 NKJV).
Drives out foolishness -- "Foolishness is bound up in the heart of a child; but the rod of correction shall drive it far from him" (Proverbs 22:15).
Calms rebellion -- "A youngster's heart is filled with rebellion, but punishment will drive it out of him" (Proverbs 22:15 Living Bible).
Delivers his soul -- "Do not withhold correction from a child for if you beat him with a rod, he will surely die. You shall beat him with a rod and deliver his soul from hell" (Proverbs 23:13-14 NKJV).
Increases his ability to learn -- "The rod and reproof give wisdom, but a child left to himself brings shame to his mother" (Proverbs 29:15 NKJV).
Quickly restores broken fellowship -- "Come and let us return unto the Lord: for he has torn, but He will heal us; He has stricken, but He will bind us up" (Hosea 6:1 NKJV).

Summary

Nurturing children is one of the most challenging Christian responsibilities. Psalm 144:12 describes the ideal result: "That our sons may be as plants grown up in youth (mature beyond their years); that our daughters may be as cornerstones (supporters of others) polished after the similitude of a palace" (having outstanding worth). The promise of this verse depends on the condition described in verse 11. "Rid me and deliver me from the hand of aliens whose mouth speaketh vanity, and their right hand is a right hand of falsehood."

Maturity comes from learning, as Moses did, to be in the world, but not of the world. We can give instruction, but, unfortunately, wisdom cannot be imposed on children. While training can prepare a child to receive the gospel and to have high moral standards, rebirth and spiritual growth are matters that cannot be enforced or inherited (John 1:12-13). Only God Himself can change a heart of stone into a heart of flesh.

Parents have a tremendous influence, but children of weak or ungodly guardians are not necessarily weak and ungodly. Manasseh, one of the most wicked kings in Judah (2 Kings 21:1-9) fathered Josiah, one of the most godly (2 Kings 22:1-2; 23:22-25). Eli, a man judged for his weakness in disciplining his own sons (1 Samuel 2:22-35) became guardian to Samuel, the prophet (1 Samuel 3:19-21). On the other hand, the children of some of the most devout believers are never regenerated. The Scriptures said of Josiah that "like unto him was there no king before him, that turned to the LORD with all his heart, and with all his soul, and with all his might, according to all the law of Moses; neither after him arose there any like him." Josiah's son Jehoahaz was an evil king (2 Kings 23:32). The prophet Samuel had sons who "walked not in his ways, but turned aside after lucre, and took bribes, and perverted judgment" (1 Samuel 8:3).

A child trained in the Scriptures is definitely set apart as privileged, but if all your children do become believers, resist taking undue credit or mentally condemning others who do not share the same joy. Salvation comes by grace and is not merited. Parents need to point the way to salvation by diligent training and example but commit the rest to our Sovereign Lord.

God holds leaders responsible for teaching His law to the next generation (Psalm 78:1-8). We are accountable to discipline those under our charge (1 Samuel 3:13). A faithful wife helps produce godly offspring for the Lord (Malachi 2:15). More faithful parents like Amram and Jochebed would transform our nation and world.

ENCOURAGING LOVE FOR CHILDREN

1. The Word challenges older women to encourage mothers to love their children (Titus 2:3). Practically speaking, how can an older woman encourage mothers?

   How can a younger woman encourage mothers?

2. Review Proverbs 31 and evaluate the Priceless Woman's characteristics as a mother. What qualities do you most need to build in your life now?

3. Contrast Proverbs 22: 6 and Proverbs 29: 15-17. How important is training?

4. Jesus demonstrated well-rounded growth (Luke 2:52). For each of the general growth areas listed below, cite at least two prayer requests for a child's healthy development.

   Intellectual

   Physical

   Spiritual

   Social

5. How can positive character qualities be encouraged in children?

6. Do you personally know a single parent, fatherless child, or a new family in your community? Pray for this parent, child or family each day this week. Look up Deuteronomy14:29 and explain the benefit God promises to believers who minister to strangers, orphans and widows.

ENCOURAGING LOVE FOR CHILDREN

"Encourage the young women to love their. . . children. . .
that the word of God may not be dishonored"
(Titus 2:4,5, NASB)

"Mom, please don't make us go back to public school!" my ten year old son, Sam, pleaded. "Couldn't you homeschool us?" The earnest look in his hazel eyes told me this was no light request. I didn't have to ask why. Sam and I both had fond memories of homeschooling his kindergarten year, even though we knew no one else who homeschooled. When Sam's natural dad became terminally ill, I enrolled him in a Christian school. After I remarried and moved to Oregon, we transferred Sam and his brother to a local government school with the reputation of one of the best in the city. As a volunteer helper in his classroom the year before, I saw otherwise. Our son had been vexed by low academic standards, disrespect for authority, and an anti-Christian curriculum. He had bravely endured, but he had valid reasons to dread returning.

Could I handle the pressure of teaching three boys at home? Could I sacrifice "my time"? For once in ten years I could finally send all of my children to school. The bus would pick them up in the morning and I could be free all day. Just think of the hours I would have undisturbed for free-lance writing, evangelism, and serving the Lord in the church. Would I have to give up my pursuits and live like an isolated hermit?

My son's request haunted me for days in my tug of war between my children's best interests and my own needs. One morning I uncovered an old issue of <u>Moody Monthly</u>, a Christian magazine. I decided to relax for a few minutes and scan the periodical before filing it away. An article on home education by Sue Welch captured my attention. Gary and I had shared excitement over this piece the year before as we planned our wedding, but we had been advised not to consider home schooling as newly-weds. We had plenty of adjustments to make as a blended family. In retrospect I'm not sure that sending the children away helped with that process. At any rate, the adjustment problem could no longer serve as an excuse. We had completed our first year of marriage. Could I home teach without jeopardizing my personal goals?

On Sunday I discovered another family at church in their second year of successful home schooling. As I witnessed their enthusiasm an older woman in the assembly joined us. Her blue eyes sparkled in the halo of her white hair as she touched my shoulder and whispered, "My dear, I wish I had known about home schooling when my children were young. I believe if you step out in faith, God will help you fulfill your greatest dreams while you nurture your children." I heeded her advice.

By shifting to home education, we made Christ central in all areas of our lives. In Him are hidden all the treasures of wisdom and knowledge. Our home was no longer fragmented by multiple schedules. The boys learned to study independently and develop initiative and personal accountability. We became each others' best friends and formed ongoing positive relationships with other home school families.

Through home school my outside ministry grew. I thought keeping the boys home would slow my development as a writer, but the first book I had published, <u>Teaching Reading at Home,</u> came as an outgrowth of principles I learned as I taught them. My oldest son even helped edit the manuscript! In doing research for our boys' school work, my husband developed an interest in history and economics. The skills Gary and I developed by home teaching led to the formation of our home business. Many of my deepest desires have come to pass because of this decision we made in faith.

I gained far more than I sacrificed when I chose to teach my own children, and our entire family has benefited. All three of our sons have successfully transitioned from homeschool to college and the work world. They have been recognized for outstanding academic achievement and commended for the ability to work harmoniously with others. As a special bonus, my husband now works at home and ministers as an elder in our church.

Godly women should seek to encourage young mothers. The specific application may not always be to encourage home schooling as the three women did in my case. But the encouragement should focus on the principle of helping children in all areas of development —mental, physical, social and spiritual.

<u>Aspects of Growth in Children</u>

Jesus modeled well-rounded physical, mental, spiritual and social growth (Luke 2:52). Parents and leaders should evaluate a child's progress in each category. Specific prayer could focus on weak areas.

1. PHYSICAL GROWTH. Physical needs, while not carrying eternal significance, do have important temporary value (1 Timothy 4:8). An individual who eats wisely and exercises regularly can have more energy to expend for the Lord in spiritual and practical areas. Likewise, if one is well-groomed she has a better testimony to the unsaved. There is always a danger for the physical areas to overly absorb one's time and thoughts. The care of the body should not be an end in itself, but a means to the end of glorifying God.

2. MENTAL GROWTH. "The fear of the Lord is the beginning of knowledge" (Proverbs 1:7a). A wise child will learn to measure all knowledge by the Word of God (Psalm 119:90-100). He will be able to view events from an eternal perspective (Hebrews 11). A teachable spirit and diligence are keys to mental growth (Proverbs 13:1;22:29). The one who learns well will be able to answer the questions of others and train them to follow the Lord (Psalm 78:4-7).

3. SPIRITUAL GROWTH. Jesus grew in favor with God and man. Spiritual development influences the ability to get along with people. Some major spiritual goals could include salvation at an early age. Although we cannot decide for a child (John 1:13), we can pray that God will provide the wisdom necessary for understanding the gospel. God promises, **"I love those who love me, and those who seek me early shall**

find me" (Proverbs 8:17). We can pray that our child will "remember now thy creator in the days of thy youth, while the evil days come not" (Ecclesiastes 12:1a). Another verse to claim for children is: "For thou art my hope, O Lord God; thou art from my trust from my youth. By thee have I been held up from the womb; thou art he who took me out of my mother; my praise shall be continually of thee" (Psalm 71:5-6).

A verse to claim for discipleship and Christian growth could include: "All thy children shall be taught of the LORD; and great shall be the peace of thy children" (Isaiah 54:13). Pray for children to have an intimate knowledge of the Word at an early age (Joshua 8:35), a worshipful heart and a thankful, joyful spirit (Psalm 148:12-13).

4. SOCIAL GROWTH. Important elements of social development include a wise choice of friends, respect for others (Leviticus 19:32), obedience and honor for parents (Eph. 6:1-3), polite behavior (Psalm 101:2a) and a forgiving spirit. "A man's wisdom gives him patience and it is His glory to overlook an offense" (Proverbs 19:11 NIV).

A key virtue to many is acceptance and popularity. Yet godly individuals need to learn, when necessary, to stand alone—to make right decisions in spite of negative pressure. Many are afraid to homeschool because they erroneously fear for their children's social development. The book in the Bible that deals the most extensively with education issues (see the repetition of words like instruction, knowledge, wisdom, and understanding) also deals in depth with social issues like chosing the right kind of friends, handling disagreements, using the tongue properly, etc. In this book called Proverbs who are the instructors and who are the pupils?

Experience shows us that peer dependence, a problem nurtured in homogeneous age group settings, can hinder healthy, personal social development. Only institutions segregate people by age groups. In the real world (the home, the neighborhood and the market place) a variety of ages harmonize. The homeschooled student grows socially through daily observing those who are more experienced and wiser while he learns to assist those who are younger or weaker. On the other hand, the child surrounded all day with peers tends to stop trying to mature because growing up could be disastrous to his social status at school. He might find it difficult to go against the crowd even if he inwardly disagrees. For survival he might learn to mistreat the unpopular.

> *He that walketh with wise men shall be wise,*
> *but a companion of fools shall be destroyed"*
> (Proverbs 13:20).

Training children requires work and vision. Many qualities for well-rounded growth can be requested in prayer. Parents or leaders of children should claim great things for the little ones. A big God appreciates large requests (Jeremiah 33:3; Eph. 3:20).

Training also necessitates correction and discipline including the use of the rod (Proverbs 10:1:17:25; 22:15, and 29:15). Parents are responsible to guide children to walk in the truth (1 Samuel 3:13). A love for our children and a concern for their long term

Encouraging Mothers

A godly woman in any stage of life should be concerned about the welfare of children. Although only a fraction of a woman's life, if at all, is spent in the active stage of child-rearing, single girls would be wise to prepare in advance for their days of motherhood and all of us should realize that a major part of the mature woman's ministry should be to encourage mothers. Youth is the promise of tomorrow, and we all share the responsibility of nurturing our most valuable resources. Mothers need all the support they can get from the Christian community. When we fail to train the younger women to love their offspring the Lord is discredited.

How can a woman train mothers to love their children?

1. EVALUATE YOUR ATTITUDE TOWARDS CHILDREN. Do we refer to children as a gift from God (Psalm 127) to treasure and train, our most valuable possessions? Or do we treat children as something to limit or avoid as a burden, a financial liability? Do we join in with jokes about finally getting kids into school and out from under foot?

The Scripture emphasizes that children are a blessing. Couples are challenged to be fruitful (Genesis 1:28; 28:3 and Psalm 128:3). Rejoice with your friend who just discovered she is pregnant with her sixth child. Biblical accounts often highlight the grief of barren couples— Abraham and Sarah, Isaac and Rebekkah, Hannah and Elkanah, Elizabeth and Zachariah, etc., but no story is recorded of a couple in the Bible distressed because they had too many.

The word blessing can be defined as a "special favor granted by God." Sometimes children seem to be anything but a blessing. We need to trust God to help us see beyond the sacrifices and disappointments, the dirty diapers of parenting. Children expose our weaknesses. They inspire growth in our lives and stretch us to accomplish things we would have never dreamed possible. Even wayward children can produce a blessing for grieving parents. One wise father of a prodigal shared how their son's sinful lifestyle drove his wife to a new depth in her devotional life. In her helplessness, she turned to the Lord for comfort and wisdom. Parents of handicapped sons or daughters often develop a beauty in their spirits that grows from unselfish, patient giving over a period of time. We need to encourage mothers to see, through the eyes of faith when necessary, that every child is a tailored designed gift from God.

2. LOVINGLY SHARE CONCERNS BUT AVOID IMPOSING YOUR PERSONAL CONVICTIONS. As a parent I have been rebuked, sometimes in critical, overbearing ways, for such things as celebrating July the 4th or Christ's birth at Christmas. The Purtains and other godly Christians chose to ignore Christmas because of the abuses of the holiday. Some, like ourselves, see opportunities to use the season to teach about our Lord. In areas such as these which are not specifically addressed in Scripture, we

might share the same ultimate goal (that Christ be glorified), yet vary in our personal application (Romans 14).

3. ENCOURAGE MOTHERS VERBALLY. What we say to mothers can greatly influence them. Words can be a powerful source of encouragement. A compliment can go a long way to lift a mother's morale (Proverbs 25:11). Be careful to praise character qualities (i.e. your child was polite today), rather than making vain remarks like, "He is so cute". Learn to evaluate a child's potential for God even when he is not being the model child. If a mother has a "brat", she probably does not need to be reminded of his problems. She needs to be inspired to help reverse the negative patterns of his life. One teacher lovingly approached the mother of a difficult child in her class by saying, "Your son has real leadership qualities. How can we work together to help him positively redirect this influence for the good of all?" Mothers need supporters and not critics.

4. GIVE MOTHERS OF YOUR TIME OR RESOURCES. Another way to encourage mothers to love their children is to practically demonstrate love for them. "I enjoy your children so much," one considerate friend told an overworked mother. "Can I have them spend an afternoon with me next week and give you a break?" By volunteering to keep the children, this woman helped the mother in two ways. First, the mother felt her own position elevated. Someone else was willing to share her responsibility. Secondly, she would feel refreshed after a break. Club leaders, baby-sitters, music teachers, tutors, and friends at church can practically encourage love for children as they contribute to their life training.

Encourage moms by providing positive resources. Pass on good books on training children or good supplies for the children themselves. Share areas of personal expertise. For example, I have experience as a reading instructor. I believe I help mothers love their children by training them to use an intensive phonetical system, a method that will help them teach their children to spell and read well. As an author, I use topics concerning home and family as an underlying theme of much of my writing.

5. PRAY FOR PARENTS AND THEIR CHILDREN. Uphold families by intercessory prayer. A woman who does not have her own children can "adopt" children for special prayer. We have an adopted grandma we have never had the joy of meeting personally, yet she faithfully prays daily for our boys. Although she lives many miles away in another country, she read about my thirty-five year old husband's death in a magazine and felt a burden for the survivors. We started corresponding years ago and the relationship grew. I regularly send her pictures of the boys and list specific prayer requests. She writes back words of encouragment. She rejoiced with me when I remarried and when the boys experience special victories. I wept with her when her beloved husband died. This very special Christian lady never had children of her own and yet because of her investment in us, she now has a godly heritage.

Some young mother out there has a void in her life you could help fill by praying for her. Key prospects might include children from single-parent families or ones who might otherwise have special needs.

Conclusion

Although the primary responsibility for training children rests on the parents, all Christians are responsible for encouraging them and reinforcing godly training. The Christian community serves as an extended family with the joint concern that children be nurtured physically, mentally, spiritually and socially.

We are exhorted to lift up families, particularly ones in positions of spiritual leadership, foreigners in our lands, and single parent households. If you minister to those with special needs, God promises a blessing in all the work of your hand (Deuteronomy 14:29). As a single parent, I felt at times overwhelmed with so many acts of kindness that I was unable to repay, but this verse gave me comfort. I did not have to personally repay my benefactors. God promised to do so Himself.

STUDY GUIDE   LESSON 17

SARAH: A WOMAN WHO MODELED PURITY

1. What do we know of Sarah's appearance (Genesis 12: 10-15)?

2. Read 1 Peter 3: 1-6 and answer the following questions:

    How can purity help a woman whose husband disobeys the Word of God?

    Does this negate the need for attention to outer deportment (1 Timothy 2:9-10)?

    How are we to imitate Sarah (Genesis 18:12)?

3. Paraphrase (write in your own words) 1 Thessalonians 4:3-6.

4. Define modesty.

    What are the benefits that come from modesty?

        for the woman herself

        for the church

        for the testimony to unbelievers

5. How does God's definition of beauty differ from the world's (Proverbs 11:22)?

6. Evaluate your own life. How can you better represent God to the world by your appearance and actions?

SARAH: A WOMAN WHO MODELED PURITY

"She maketh herself coverings of tapestry; her clothing is silk and purple. . . .
Strength and honour are her clothing; and she shall rejoice in time to come"
(Proverbs 31:22b, 25)

Sarah's beauty captivated men. The Bible refers to her as "very fair" and "lovely to look upon." Her gorgeous appearance caused her husband Abraham to fear for his life when they sojourned in a foreign country. Other men might destroy him so they could claim her for themselves (Genesis 12:10-15). An Egyptian ruler coveted Sarah even when she was ninety years old (Genesis 20:1-18).

"You have become her children [daughters of Sarah] if you do what is right without being frightened by any fear" (1 Peter 3:6b, NASB). In what way are we encouraged to pattern after Sarah? Does this mean we need to be alluring, sensual and beautiful to be loved? Advertisers plant that idea in our minds. Buy their product and we will have the desire of our hearts. We crave compliments on our appearance. We spend hours shopping for the perfect dress, fixing our hair and applying make-up. We purchase the perfume that promises to intrigue men. Sarah's example corrects several erroneous ideas about true beauty.

Godly Beauty Grows from Inside Out

Pretty clothes and careful grooming are not wrong. Like Sarah, the Proverbs 31 woman cared for her outer appearance, but her confidence did not rest in transient externals. She won praise from others for her inner qualities. The admonition to copy Sarah cannot refer to traits over which we have no control. Many women are not and never will be physically beautiful. Artificial attempts to disguise reality will not change the facts. But we can all copy Sarah. The Scripture explains:

> "Even if some do not obey the word, they, without a word, may be won by the conduct of their wives, when they observe your chaste conduct accompanied by fear.
>
> Do not let your beauty be that outward adorning of arranging the hair, of wearing gold, or of putting on fine apparel; but let it be the hidden person of the heart, with the incorruptible ornament of a gentle and quiet spirit, which is very precious in the sight of God.
>
> For in this manner, in former times, the holy women who trusted in God also adorned themselves, being submissive to their own husbands, as Sarah obeyed Abraham, calling him lord, whose daughters you are if you do good and are not afraid with any terror. "
>
> (1 Peter 3:1b-6 NKJV)

A Meek and Quiet Spirit Seeks to Glorify God, Not Self

Today, four thousand years later, we can only imagine how Sarah looked. No photographs preserve her beauty. The radiance of her face has faded. Her body has decayed, and she is remembered primarily as a woman of faith (Hebrews 11:11).

What characteristics of God can a daughter of Sarah represent to the world?

1. GOD IS LOVE. A woman who controls her sensual powers models love, thereby using her life to strengthen others (Romans 12:1). God created men and women differently. A man becomes aroused by the sight of a woman's body and the woman is excited by his excitement. He wants to look; she wants to allure. Within marriage the visual stimulation should give mutual pleasure, but tight or skimpy clothing which accentuates the female body should be saved for the bedroom. Outside of marriage sexual enticement is sinful. Jesus warns men that lust is like the sin of adultery (Matthew 5:27-28). Therefore it is important for a woman to remain modest in public while feeling free to model for her husband in private.

A chaste, pure woman can draw others to the Savior (1 Peter 3:1-2). As women we can either choose to highlight our female body by wearing teasing or revealing clothes or we can choose to draw attention to our soul and to our Lord.

2. GOD IS HOLY. We should be careful to portray His holy character with tasteful clothes and discreet behavior. An immodest woman tempts or defrauds others by teasing with something they cannot rightfully have. A woman's presence should uplift and edify, not serve as a snare. Sometimes women blindly cause men to stumble because of insensitivity or ignorance on what creates problems for men.

What does tempt a brother to have impure thoughts? In an effort to answer this question, my late husband polled a cross-section of Christian men. He selected anonymous participants from a wide range of categories: single, married, new believers, church leaders, teenagers and grandfathers. He discovered an amazing level of consistency in their opinions. Some of the findings are as follows:

a. **Godly men want to avoid lustful thoughts.** Godly men think differently than the world commonly teaches. In contrast to the image of men joyfully getting an eyeful, Christian brothers desire purity of thought. They try to train themselves to "study a woman's face and not her body." The men want "more sisters in the Lord and less objects," and they commend the ladies who show "consideration for the peace of mind of men." One hoped that "the women would realize the great potential they have for causing men to stumble by the way they dress or act." He longs for "sensitivity and a willingness to sacrifice rights for the benefit of the men."

The men surveyed felt women need teaching in this area. One brother said, "Older women should counsel young girls." Some mentioned the need for "a general awareness of what is distracting and what is modest," observing that, "some older women in leadership need counseling themselves." Several commented that some Christian sisters, perhaps without knowing it, dress like harlots.

b. All men can be tempted. Although the mature Christian man has the spiritual resources to combat impure thoughts, he is still vulnerable to temptation. Many have lost spiritual vitality because of an impure thought life. We should be considerate, remembering that "the eyes of a man are never satisfied" (Proverbs 27:20b).

c. Sexual excitement is not the medium for producing love. Sexual power can be used temporarily to draw some men, but cannot sustain a meaningful relationship. Many women erroneously believe that lust is flattering attention. A woman may be deceived if she feels sexual attraction is a basis for her worth as an individual. Any woman can be the object of lust. Beauty is not needed; men can be tempted by unattractive women. Personal value is not necessary; a lewd photograph of a stranger can excite a man.

3. GOD IS ORDERLY. While a Christain woman should not dress like a harlot, she should take care in her appearance. A believer manifests God's character by, as much as possible, maintaining well groomed hair and nails, a healthy body, and neat apparel.

The Creator God also designed things with specific purposes. In the heavens He made the greater light to rule the day and the lesser light to rule the night. Among mankind He created a chain-of-command for social order. A daughter of Sarah finds satisfaction and joy in her God-given feminine role.

The Egyptian ruler clearly recognized Sarah as a woman. For her to have dressed like a man would have been distasteful to Abimelech and an abomination to God (Deuteronomy 22:5). How would a woman dress in those days? Both male and female Hebrews wore long garments, but women wore theirs loose and flowing while men girded their loins in a manner that freed them for fighting in battle and doing more aggressive tasks. See 2 Kings 1:8, Job 38:3, 40:7; Isaiah 5:27, and Jeremiah 13:11. Today, how can a woman dress as distinctly female? It is good to ask ourselves, "If a stranger would see us coming from a distance, could he tell if we are male or female?"

4. GOD IS AN ARTISTIC BEING. Daughters of Sarah serve the Originator of color, rich variety, and orderly design. The recommended color of clothing is never prescribed in Scripture, but knowing the nature of God should make us question the practice of restricting dress to dull, drab shades. He made the flowers of the field using variations of color blends—deep tones, light pastels, combinations of the two. In the Sermon on the Mount Jesus compares the clothing He wants to provide for us with the lilies of the field (Matthew 6:28-30).

Modesty does not mean drab or dumpy. Some people teach that a godly woman cannot wear any make-up, her dresses must be black or dull in color and her hair must be straight and plain. To them jewelry, even a wedding ring, is unacceptable. They miss the main point of 1 Peter 3.

Peter checks the heart against pride about outward appearances. He taxes vanity. Ironically, some who dress austerely have false piety. We should not exaggerate the meaning of modesty (i.e. only long dresses an inch above the ankles) or legislate asceticism (i.e. only plain, ordinary garments). Severe clothing is often associated with cults and not necessarily godliness. While make-up or jewelry might be offensively overdone, Scripture does not restrict all use of make-up or forbid wedding rings.

Abraham sent gifts of jewelry to the future bride for his son (Genesis 24:22). A wedding ring is not designed to allure. A ring symbolizes the marriage bond and announces that a woman is reserved for one man. The point of 1 Peter is to explain that jewelry, hairdos and clothing selections do not make the woman. We should not spend undue energy or time on fashion while ignoring the inner qualities that produce lasting beauty.

Summary

Sarah's beauty source surpassed man-made coverings. Her attraction did not stem from artificial means like exotic hairdos, expensive jewelry, or sensual clothing. She inwardly adorned herself with the imperishable quality of a gentle and quiet spirit, which is precious in the sight of God (1 Peter 3:3-6a). Sarah was neat and attractive, but her lasting appeal flowed primarily out of an inner walk with God that penetrated her outer appearance to soften her face and give her a lovely radiance.

As women we need to pray for guidance from the Holy Spirit as we select our wardrobe. We can evaluate each outfit by the question, "To what is the attention drawn?" Color combinations and clothing styles should highlight the face, the doorway to the soul. We can avoid make-up or outfits that are overpowering or draw attention away from the inner person (1 Timothy 2:9). An honorable style of dress accentuates godly character.

Some women dress in a way that announces a discontented, restless, roving spirit, seeking to allure men. Other women reveal openly their rejection of their submissive, feminine role. Their aggressive manners and masculine clothing proclaim their competitive mind-set. Some women focus on drawing attention to themselves by their outward appearance. Their flashy and loud exterior may be an attempt to hide a shallow, undernourished soul. Some women pride themselves in their austere or sloppy dress.

Few women are daughters of Sarah, feminine women who humbly seek to honor God in the sensitive, personal area of dress. Christian women, following Sarah's example, ought to live holy lives so that they can teach others to be discreet (careful in their words and actions) and chaste (modest and moral), in order that the Lord will not be disgraced (Titus 2:3-5). We should ask ourselves, "What kind of advertisement are we for the Christian faith?"

STUDY GUIDE   LESSON 18

ENCOURAGING PURITY

1. Contrast the women described in Proverbs 7 and Proverbs 31.

	Proverbs 7:5-27	Proverbs 31:10-31
moral standards		
dress		
speech		
relationship with God		
goals in life		
effect on others		

2. How does Proverbs 5:18-19 reveal the pleasure God intends for married people?

    How does Satan try to pervert this experience (Proverbs 5:15-20; Matthew 5:27-28)?

    Give some reasons why we should save sexual intimacy for marriage
    (1 Corinthians 6:18-20; Ephesians 5:31; and Hebrews 13:4).

3. Although the Scriptures honor marriage (1 Corinthians 7:2-6), what are the avantages
    of being single (1 Corinthians 7:28-40)? Why?

4. The Proverbs 7 woman dressed like a harlot (v.10). How does a harlot dress?
    (Optional: Ask a couple of men for their opinion.)

5. Why would a woman practice impurity? List excuses some give. What Scriptures
    can you name to help refute the "vain deceiving words"?

6. Explain the benefits of a pure, virtuous life.

ENCOURAGING PURITY

"Older women likewise are to be reverent in their behavior. . . teaching what is good,
that they may encourage the young women to be sensible, pure. . .
that the word of God may not be dishonored.
(Titus 2:3-5, NASB)

One elderly woman, a patient in a rest home, had few of the trappings associated with worldly beauty. Wrinkles lined her face as she lay dying of cancer. But a gentleness of spirit softened the marks of time. Her light blue nightgown matched her blue eyes which twinkled as she spoke of her Savior.

My first husband, a young medic doing volunteer work in the facility, visited her room. After twenty minutes in her presence he felt so impressed by her glowing countenance that he declared, "Rarely have I met a woman so beautiful." He drove fifty miles to get me, his young bride, and bring me to meet this stranger who had captivated his soul. **Together we agreed that an aged body could not destroy the inner radiance that shone through her face.** Her beauty stemmed from a pure life poured out in service to others. Years after this lady has gone to be with the Lord, her memory lingers. The impact of her life continues to bless.

In the next bed of the same nursing facility another patient represented a different way of life. Dyed red hair encircled a heavily made up face. The caked on blue eye shadow could not disguise the deep, hard lines around her eyes. Large earrings dangled and her low-cut see-through gown revealed sagging breasts. Once a woman of outward beauty, her personage now was repugnant like a wilted flower in smelly water. She yelled at the nurses, her voice bitter and hostile. Nothing seemed to satisfy her. Others avoided her company.

Contrasting Two Women in Proverbs

As I compared these two women I could not help but wonder about their lives in earlier days. What were they like in their youth? They reminded me of two different types of women in the book of Proverbs.

The Proverbs 31 woman, like the first woman in the rest home, focuses her energies on her inner character, her walk with God. The other woman in Proverbs lives a sensuous life. In her power she draws men to herself. "But in the end she is bitter as gall, sharp as a double-edged sword. Her feet go down to death" (Proverbs 5:4-5). The two women make a valuable contrast. Men felt attracted to them both, but for different reasons and with different results.

Proverbs 7 / The Sensuous Woman	Proverbs 31 / The Godly Woman
immoral, common, cheap (v.5)	virtuous, rare, valuable (v.10)
dresses like a harlot (v.10)	clothed with dignity (v.25)
crafty, uses others (v.10)	helps others (v.20)
loud and defiant, never stays home (v.11)	content, responsible homemaker (v.27)
uses religion to cover deceit (v.14)	fears the Lord (v.30)
depends on sensual allurements (v.17)	depends on inner development (v.30)
lives for the moment (v.18)	looks to future (v.25)
deceitful (v.19)	trustworthy (v.11)
seduces with smooth talk (v.21)	speaks with wisdom (v.26)
victimizes / destroys strong men (v.26)	strengthens, builds strong leaders (v.23)
provides temporary pleasure (v.18)	blesses lives (v.28)
but ultimately destroys (v.27)	brings good not harm (v.12)

Viewing Sex from God's Perspective

The pure woman recognizes God's purpose for intimacy. He divinely created the sexual expression of love as a bonding seal between a husband and wife, physically demonstrating the spiritual joining of two separate hearts (Ephesians 5:31). The man is to love his wife even as himself and the wife is to reverence her husband (Ephesians 5:33) and yield to him (Ephesians 5:22). This union is the most delicate of all human relationships. Consequently, God created the conjugal union in marriage to be an ecstatic experience, a precious, private, unique expression of mutual commitment. A married woman need not be timid before her husband. Her body belongs to him (1 Corinthians 7:2-5) and is designed to provide blessing, joy, satisfaction and exhilaration (Proverbs 5:15-19). "Marriage is honorable in all, and the bed undefiled" (Hebrews 13:4).

1. MISUSES OF SEX. Sacred things can be abused and sex is no exception. We live in an age of instant self-gratification, but haste to secure this gift robs it of its beauty. God did not design sex for personal pleasure at the expense of others. Outside of marriage, sexual excitement is lowered from an elevated, hallowed experience to a passing fling that leaves one guilt-ridden, empty, vulnerable, and disillusioned. A woman who flaunts her body lessens her beauty. Proverbs 11:22 states: "Like a ring of gold in a swine's snout, so is a fair woman which is without discretion."

2. TEMPORAL NATURE OF SEX. The sexual expression, although gratifying in marriage, is not the ultimate joy. The human institution of marriage is only for this life. "The time is short," warns the apostle Paul. "From now on even those who have wives should be as though they had none. . . for the form of this world is passing away" (1 Corinthians 7:29, 31, NKJV). Sex is a temporary pleasure. Only a deep personal relationship with Jesus fully satisfies (Psalm 73:25-26). Therefore our major goal—whether married, single, or single again—should be to prepare to be His bride, "a

glorious church, not having spot, or wrinkle, or any such thing; but that it should be holy and without blemish" (Ephesians 5:27). The unmarried Christian has the advantage of being free to concentrate on the Lord in an undivided way (1 Corinthians 7:7-9, 32-34).

Answering Excuses for Immodesty or Immorality

Satan is a liar and the father of all lies. He made Eve think God was withholding pleasure and satisfaction when He restricted one type of fruit. Satan is in the same business today of casting doubt in our minds about God's love. Let us see from the Word how God counters Satan's accusations concerning modest dress and purity of action.

1. "EVERYONE IS DOING IT." The virtuous woman spoken of in Proverbs 31:10 is rare. A woman can choose to be a precious jewel or a dime-store trinket. Christians are admonished not to be "conformed to this world" (Romans 12:2) and to "walk no longer just as the Gentiles also walk... because of the ignorance that is in them and they... have given themselves over to sensuality" (Ephesians 4:17-19 NASB). The beauty of the one-flesh experience was not designed for experimentation outside of a marriage commitment.

2. "EVERYONE WILL THINK I'M A SQUARE." We are challenged to be trend setters, not robots subject to the whims of clothing designers or television stars. We are responsible to be an "example of the believers in word.. in purity" (1 Timothy 4:12).

3. "I'M FREE TO DO AS I PLEASE." True freedom is self-control over temptation to sin. "While they promise them liberty, they themselves are the servants of corruption: for of whom a man is overcome, of the same is he brought in bondage" (2 Peter 2:19). One with true freedom considers the rights of others. "For brethren, ye have been called unto liberty; only use not liberty for an occasion to the flesh, but by love serve one another" (Galatians 5:13).

4. "IT DOESN'T HURT ANYBODY." The Scriptures as well as experience verify the fallacy of this reasoning. It is recorded, "she hath cast down many wounded; yea, many strong men have been slain by her" (Proverbs 7:26). "She also lieth in wait as for a prey and increaseth the transgressors among men" (Proverbs 23:28).

5. "THAT'S HIS PROBLEM." Like it or not, we are our brother's keeper. Paul makes our accountability clear in 1 Thessalonians 4:3-6 NKJV. "This is the will of God, your sanctification: that you should abstain from sexual immorality; that each of you should know how to possess his own vessel in sanctification and honor, not in passion of lust, like the Gentiles who do not know God; that no one should take advantage of and defraud his brother in this matter, because the Lord is the avenger of all such."

6. "I'LL MISS OUT ON ALL THE FUN." Lasting pleasure brings peaceable results. The fruits of the Spirit (Galatians 5:22-23) are contrasted with lust (Gal. 5:19-21). The fruit of sensuality is defilement, not fun (Mark 7:21-23). Sex is not a life essential.

Even in marriage there will be necessary periods of abstinence for illness or pregnancy. Couples may be separated because of jobs, wartime or other commitments.

7. "MY FRIEND DOES, AND SHE'S A CHRISTIAN." We have to account for ourselves to God individually (Romans 14:10,12; 2 Corinthians 5:10).

Considering Some Benefits for Purity and Modesty

The world entices us to misuse sexual allurements, but God desires to protect us. When a woman controls and sanctifies her body, she receives many blessings.

1. HER CHRISTIAN TESTIMONY IS ENHANCED. "That we may lead a quiet and peaceable life in all godliness and reverence for this is good and acceptable in the sight of God our Savior. . . . Therefore I desire that the men pray everywhere, lifting up holy hands, without wrath and doubting; in like manner also, that the women adorn themselves in modest apparel, with propriety and moderation, not with braided hair or gold or pearls or costly clothing, but which is proper for women professing godliness, with good works" (1 Timothy 2:2-3, 8-10 NKJV). The testimony of a godly woman speaks honorably for the Lord.

2. MEN ARE FREED FOR STRONGER SPIRITUAL VITALITY. Modest women contribute positively to public worship (1 Timothy 2:8-9). Instead of being teased or tempted to sin, men are free to concentrate on their spiritual responsibilities of leadership in prayer and worship.

3. OTHERS ARE NOT LED INTO SIN. The godly woman does not "market her goods" to those who cannot rightly receive them. She does not violate the heart of another by stimulating or arousing them sexually for her own self-pleasure.

4. THE WOMAN IS HONORED AND PROTECTED. The modest woman will inspire protection from men. The impure woman plays up to a man's fallen nature and is more likely to be abused (Romans 8:5-6). "Why is it," asked a collegiate notorious for her immodesty, "that all the men seem to want of me is my body?" This girl, a Christian who spent hours in Bible study, expressed a desire to marry a mature Christian. Instead she drew the attention of men who would exploit her.

5. SHE IS ABLE TO ENJOY LOVE MORE DEEPLY. Much is lost when a woman spreads herself widely. A chaste woman preserves love's full force. The teaching in Proverbs applies to women as well as men: "Drink water from your own cistern, running water from your own well. Should your springs overflow in the streets, your streams of water to be shared with strangers" (Proverbs 5:15-18).

6. SHE CAN CONCENTRATE ON THINGS OF LASTING VALUE. God does not take pleasure in physical beauty (Proverbs 31:30) which fades. The Lord takes pleasure in those who fear Him, in those who hope in His mercy (Psalm 147:11).

<u>Ways to Avoid Impurity</u>

We are not immune to sexual temptation. But the work of the cross can deliver us from the power of sin over our lives. Temptation is not sin, but to entertain lustful thoughts and/or actions is. There are ways to break the hold of sin.

1. TRANSFORM THINKING TO HARMONIZE WITH GOD'S (Romans 12:1-2). Recognize the sinfulness of impurity (whether flirting, lustful fantasy, immodesty or immorality). Satan's first trick is to redefine terms. Immodesty becomes "in style." Adultery becomes "an interlude, a fling, liaison, or a love affair". Satan makes sin romantic, or amusing, while he disguises the consequences: corrosion of trust, broken relationships, remorse, fear of discovery and guilt. Trust God and His proven character over Satan's enticing (but temporary) thrills. Sin is never worth the price. Turn fantasies over to Christ. Allow Him to take thoughts captive (2 Corinthians 10:5). Confess sins, forsake them and draw nigh to God so Satan will flee (James 4:7).

2. MAKE NO PROVISION FOR THE FLESH (Romans 13:12b-14). Evaluate reading and viewing habits. Avoid situations and activities designed to stimulate or arouse sexual impulses. If need be, sever detrimental relationships. Feeding fleshly fantasies promotes dissatisfaction with God's provision.

3. CONSECRATE DIVINELY GIVEN SEX INSTINCT IN SERVICE TO GOD. (1 Corinthians 7:34). Channel surplus energy in positive directions. Work with children, older people, or anyone needing tenderness and love. Exercise or find creative outlets in music, the arts or in some skill area.

4. DELIGHT IN POSITIVE ASPECTS OF PURITY. Work from the inside out. Concentrate on building inner character that will not fade. Claim Philippians 4:8-9: "Whatsoever things are true... whatsoever things are pure... if there be any virtue think on these things... and the God of peace shall be with you."

<u>Conclusion</u>

True holiness does not mean suppressed joy. God does not deprive; He frees us for greater pleasures, for deeper satisfactions than the thrill of flirting and getting a response.

A pure woman, of whatever age, provides a fragrant aroma to a dying world (Ephesians 5:1-9). When believers practice purity there is more love, greater harmony, and increased power that come from clear consciences. The unsaved community is drawn to the Savior who is capable of satisfying the deepest needs.

PRISCILLA: A WOMAN WHO WORKED AT HOME

1. Describe the relationship between Priscilla, Aquila and Paul (Acts 18:1-3).

   Aquila and Priscilla moved to spread the gospel to Ephesus. Describe how they used their home for God (Acts 18:18-28). What resulted from their ministry?

2. Identify another way this couple used their home (1 Corinthians 16:19). How might this be done today?

3. In 56 A.D. Priscilla and Aquila moved back to Rome. What possible risk might have been involved in this move (Acts 18:2)?

   How did they use their home in this country (Romans 16:3-5a)?

   Review the information we know about this couple. Imagine yourself in their shoes, moving four times, constantly opening their lives to others. What types of sacrifices did Priscilla make in her commitment to use her home for the Lord?

   What will be some of her eternal rewards?

4. Priscilla helped her husband in his home industry. Name some creative alterna tives for women today to supplement the family income without seeking outside employment.

5. Define hospitality. Contrast true hospitality with "entertaining". What excuses do you make for not showing hospitality? Which of these are linked with pride?

6. How can you use your room, or home in ministry to your family and others? Is there someone you feel led to open your home to this week? If so plan to make a specific invitation.

PRISCILLA: A WOMAN WHO WORKED AT HOME

"She watches over the ways of her household and
does not eat the bread of idleness."
(Proverbs 31:27 NKJV).

The hut lacked the splendor of some of the magnificent buildings in ancient Corinth. Priscilla and Aquila sat at their roughly-hewn table. A single clay lamp lit the barren room that housed both home and shop. Folded tents leaned against mud-daubed walls. Simple surroundings, however, did not restrict a mighty work for God. A "Better Homes and Gardens" atmosphere is not necessary for a home to be a center of ministry.

This couple fled Rome when Claudius ordered all Jews to leave. Paul, likewise a tentmaker by trade, sought them out. He stayed and worked with them (Acts 18:1-3). The Apostle made tents for a living, but devoted himself after work to preaching and testifying to Jews that Jesus was the Messiah. We do not know if Paul helped convert Priscilla and Aquila, but it is apparent that he discipled them in the faith.

In 53 A.D., two years after they met Paul, the couple moved with him to join his missionary outreach to Ephesus. They remained there alone while Paul ventured forth to other areas. Later they risked their lives to return to the land from which they had been exiled.

How Did Aquila and Priscilla Used Their Home for God?

1. AQUILA AND PRISCILLA BOARDED THE APOSTLE PAUL, They provided lodging for Paul (Acts 18:3). Housing him in Ephesus probably meant crowds in their home late into the evening (Acts 20:7, 11). Their popular guest had enemies as well as friends. Caring for him involved dangers. Paul personally expressed thankfulness, admitting that these fellow workers, " risked their own necks for my life, to whom not only I give thanks, but also all the churches of the Gentiles" (Romans 16:3 NKJV). We can only guess what perils they faced, but we do know their sacrifice advanced the cause of Christ.

2. AQUILA AND PRISCILLA HOSTED THE MEETING OF THE CHURCH. Repeatedly they housed successful pioneer church ministries. Believers collectively gathered in their home to worship. Priscilla faced extra hours of cleaning and rearranging furniture to accommodate groups. She opened her life and home to the scrutiny of others. One missionary who hosted a church in her home confessed that she had no secrets. Others looked in her cupboards, her closets, her dressers. She lived an exposed, transparent life.

This dedicated couple, committed to the establishment of new churches, relocated several times. These moves required courage and flexibility. Each time they moved, they endured the insecurity attached to culture shock and the stigma of being a foreigner. They moved from Rome (Acts 18:2), to Corinth (1 Corinthians 16:19), to Ephesus (Acts 18:19), back to Rome (Romans 16:3,5) and finally back to Ephesus (2 Timothy 4:19). They surrendered their rights to worldly roots and stability for the opportunity to serve the Lord.

3. AQUILA AND PRISCILLA INSTRUCTED THE LEADER APOLLOS. Within the context of their home, Priscilla assisted her husband in instructing Apollos. Their ministry produced a positive change in Apollos' leadership. "He greatly helped those who had believed by grace; for he vigorously refuted the Jews publicly, showing from the Scriptures that Jesus is the Christ" (Acts 18:27b-28 NKJV). Apollos developed as one of the most outstanding leaders of his day (1 Corinthians 3:6).

4. PRISCILLA HELPED HER HUSBAND IN MAKING TENTS (Acts 18:3). An enterprising woman, by working from within the home, Priscilla resourcefully redeemed the time without detracting from family priorities. In a similar way the virtuous woman in Proverbs made crafts at home which she sold to the merchants (Proverbs 31:24).

Modern feminists use Priscilla as an example of a career woman. Mary Pride in her book, The Way Home, points out several problems with this interpretation:

> 1) Tentmaking is a home crafts business. It is nothing like getting into a car, driving fifteen minutes across town, parking, walking into an office building, staying there for eight or nine hours, and then driving home. You don't go to the office to make tents. Not in first century Europe.
> 2) No children are ever mentioned. Because of Priscilla and Aquila's extreme mobility some commentators assume they had no children. This is only an assumption, but it's worth mentioning.
> 3) Aquila was a tentmaker, and Priscilla worked with him. Their business was not Priscilla's independent operation.
>
> All that can be said from Priscilla's example is that it is certainly fine for married Christian women to help their husbands with their home businesses. No word here of day-care for tots or nine-to-five outside careers. [1]

What Are Some Creative Alternatives to Working Outside the Home?

Like Priscilla, we can supplement the family income without seeking outside employment. A married woman working outside faces special problems which can be avoided. A working wife often returns home from work exhausted from the stress and pressure of the outside world. Instead of ministering to her family, she needs to be upheld and strengthened herself. The torn loyalty between two heads, her husband and her boss, can cause resentments to build. Family needs may become burdensome.

Daily interaction outside can increase the lust for material possessions, yet the financial gain from a second income can be deceiving. One woman after calculating job-related expenses (outside meals, higher taxes, extra social security payments, union dues, child-care, transportation, clothing and so forth), realized that from her high-paying full time job, she only netted twenty-five dollars a week!

The increase in broken homes in America has paralleled the increase in married women working outside the home. Up until the Industrial Revolution men provided for the family. With World War II and the Korean Conflict, women began migrating from the home to the office or factory. This trend escalated even after these national emergencies dwindled. Simultaneously marriage suffered as an institution. In 1780 one marriage in thirty-three ended in divorce in America. By 1955 the ratio had changed to one in four and by the 1980's the divorce rate had increased to almost one out of two.

A woman working on her own schedule, rather than in a 40 hour a week job away from home, is free to put her family first, redeeming spare times to develop supplemental cash. Home businesses fall into three categories: teaching a skill, offering a service, or providing a product.

1. TEACHING A SKILL. Teaching could include tutoring children, conducting a class on cooking or exercise, giving music lessons, or other specialized assistance. Teaching foreign immigrants English as a second language can help build cross-cultural friendships as well as meet a need. As a service to families who want to home school but would appreciate a weekly break where someone else supplemented the education, provide a "one day school."

2. OFFERING A SERVICE. A service might include child-care, hair styling, altering clothes, preparing income tax forms, refinishing furniture, bookkeeping, secretarial assistance or providing pet care while people go on vacations. One woman set up a room in her home for a word processor. During her toddler's nap time she typed manuscripts for professional people. At the hours when she could not work she rented the use of her room and processor to other women who wanted part-time employment.

3. PROVIDING A PRODUCT. A product may be home baked fruitcakes, home sewn goods, original art work, floral arrangements, or decorated cakes. A woman can barter or sell pattern designs to craft magazines or do free-lance writing. One Christian woman decorated homemade items with Scripture messages. When she received more orders than she could fill, she gave other women projects on consignment.

Sometimes a woman can combine all three areas. For example, a woman might teach a class in decorating and sell the cakes she made for the demonstration. Then she might write a how-to-article for a woman's magazine illustrated by photographs of her original cake design.

The Ministry Potential of the Home

The home is more than the core of family life. It can be the hub of a woman's outreach ministry. Through hospitality, a woman can either encourage saints or evangelize unsaved contacts (3 John 5,8). Dawson Trotman, the founder of the Christian service group called the Navigators, said, **"I believe with all my heart that one of the greatest soul-saving stations in the world is the home."** 2 The need for opening the home is so crucial that being "given to hospitality" is a requirement for married men in positions of leadership (1 Timothy 3:2). Wives of leaders must help them fulfill this responsibility.

Homemaking is more than a perfection of skills in culinary art and other aspects of home economics. Hosting is more than serving lavish meals in an elegant setting. A proper heart puts people before self. Karen Burton Mains helps define true hospitality in contrast to entertaining.

> *Entertaining has little to do with real hospitality. Secular entertaining is a terrible bondage. Its source is human pride. Demanding perfection, fostering the urge to impress, it is a rigorous taskmaster which enslaves. In contrast, Scriptural hospitality is a freedom which liberates.*

> *Entertaining says, "I want to impress you with my beautiful home, my clever decorating, my gourmet cooking." Hospitality, however, seeks to minister. It says, "This home is not mine. It is truly a gift from my Master. I am His servant and I use it as He desires." Hospitality does not try to impress, but to serve.*

> *Entertaining always puts things before people.... Hospitality, however, puts people before things.... Because hospitality has put away its pride, it doesn't care if other people see our humanness. Because we are maintaining no false pretensions, people relax and feel that perhaps we can be friends.... Entertaining subtly declares, "This is mine... Look, please, and admire." Hospitality whispers, "What is mine is yours." Entertaining looks for a payment.... Hospitality does everything with no thought of reward, but takes pleasure in the joy of giving, doing, loving, serving.* [3]

Conclusion

Priscilla set the example of opening her home to individuals like Paul and Apollos, and to groups of believers. Christian women today can continue to advance God's kingdom by practicing hospitality. Some involved in pioneer church planting situations can, like Priscilla, host a house church. Others may host small Bible study groups, prayer meetings, or evangelistic neighborhood studies. We extend hospitality to visiting missionaries or guests at church. When believers allow their homes to be a dynamic center of ministry the Lord's name is exalted (Titus 2:3-5) and people's lives are changed.

1 Pride, Mary. <u>The Way Home: Beyond Feminism, Back to Reality</u>. Crossway Books: Westchester, Illinois, 1985, p. 144. Used with permission.

2 Trotman, Dawson, <u>Born to Reproduce</u> (Lincoln Nebraska: Back to the Bible Broadcast, 1975), p.18. Used with permission.

3 Mains, Karen Burton, <u>Open Heart- Open Home</u>. (Elgin, Illinois: David C. Cook Publishing Co.,1976), pp. 25-26. Used with permission.

ENCOURAGING HOMEWORKING

1. Review Proverbs 31:10-31. Evaluate the responsibilities she supervises in the home. What domestic skills has she developed?

   Find expressions that reveal the satisfaction she feels in managing her home. How do we see home commitments taking priority over community outreach?

2. A woman must learn to budget. What are the dangers of buying items on credit (Proverbs 22:7; Romans 13:8)?

3. Share some budgeting secrets you have learned.

4. What role does attitude play in keeping the home?

   Proverbs 15:17, 17:1

   Proverbs 21:19; 25:24; 27;15

   Proverbs 24:3-4

5. Paraphrase Proverbs 14:1.

   What are some ways a woman can wisely build a house? How can she tear her house down?

   Many women are bored and frustrated as homemakers. Others are stimulated and challenged by the role. Explain the difference.

6. How can you practically encourage others to be keepers at home?

ENCOURAGING HOMEWORKING

"That they may teach the young women... to be keepers at home...
that the Word of God be not blasphemed"
(Titus 2:4-5).

I longed to stay home and learn to keep house, but as a young bride I felt I had to work. My husband Steve taught one class of English with a teaching fellowship and went to graduate school full time. How could we survive without my income?

Over Christmas break I contracted a viral infection. At Easter I still carried a low grade fever. The doctor hospitalized me. After extensive testing, he decided I needed rest. He recommended we find another teacher to finish out the remaining six-weeks of the 1971-72 school year. The change was wonderful for me, but hard for our budget. Without warning we lost three-fourths of our income.

Should Steve drop out of school? We decided to see if we could manage on the $250 a month he made part-time. Much to our surprise, a great deal of my income went to social security, taxes and job related expenses. It costs less to stay at home. We thought we had lived frugally, but we identified many non-essentials. We cancelled newspaper and magazine subscriptions and decided to utilize the public library more. Much of my salary went to pay other people to do services I could perform. I learned to cut our hair, sew, and bake from scratch. We dusted off our bicycles for a more economical and healthy means of local transportation. Picnics in the park replaced weekly steak dinners in a fancy restaurant.

New joy and peace made up for lost luxuries. Cooking became fun. Instead of the rush each night to get something quickly on the table, I calmly prepared the evening meal and warmly greeted my mate. For the first time, I was available to focus on his needs.

Although I recovered in time to resume teaching in the fall, I resigned. We decided that we needed me in the home more than the money I could make outside the home. We began to question the statement we so often heard from others. "I wish I could stay home like you, but we can't afford it." We had thought we couldn't afford it, but we creatively lived eighteen months on a part-time income. We never asked anyone for money. We paid all our bills on time and ate something nutritious for every meal.

The benefits of our experience increased over the years. Necessity taught me thrift and resourcefulness. I discovered contentment with fewer material possessions. The challenge to live on less helped prepare me for other times of low income. We survived two months between jobs with no pay, a term as missionaries with no guaranteed salary, and four years in full-time Christian work. Steve had no life insurance when he left me a widow with three small boys. Through it all I remained a full-time keeper at home.

My church gave me regular fellowship and surprise gifts of time and money.

Recognizing the Need

A woman's presence in the home is irreplaceable. A homemaker is one who changes a house into a home. Many of her jobs could be performed by others. A dry cleaners could process laundry, a restaurant serve meals, an interior decorator stylishly furnish a dwelling, and a maid complete menial tasks, but only a homemaker can add that intangible quality that money cannot buy.

All women to some degree have the job of homemaker—for a mate, a child, a relative, female roommate, or even for themselves. Anyone has a room or corner of a room over which she presides. Karen, a single girl living with her parents, demonstrates that attitudes necessary for happy, successful homemaking are universally adaptable. She tastefully decorated her room and makes others feel welcome. Discouraged friends and family members retreat to her bedroom. In her secular job she seeks to develop skills and character qualities that will help her succeed as a full-time homemaker some day.

Many women who once worked outside of the home admit that the job of homemaking is more challenging than their previous career. The homemaker needs initiative and self-motivation for her diversified job. As an executive administrator she has no time card to punch and no foreman to give instructions or supervise her work.

The creative homemaker recognizes the value of her job and constantly seeks to improve her skills. We will evaluate some of her areas of responsibility such as overall organization, budgeting, meal planning and decorating.

Organizing the Home

There are a number of key principles in organizing a home. Order makes true flexibility possible. When time is not organized the chores dominate the woman, but with a workable schedule, she can master the chores.

1. CLEAN OUT UNNECESSARY POSSESSIONS. Do not horde. The items that "may come in handy some day" clutter closets and drawers and complicate life. Freedom comes from streamlining possessions. If it has not been opened, cooked with, sat on, squeezed into, read, or watered in the last year, it probably will never be needed. Give it away to someone who will use it (Proverbs 14:21). One woman decided not to save hand-me-downs for the children she "might" have. When she did have a third child the Lord provided nicer things than before. Literally, she saw a fulfillment of the promise, "The liberal soul shall be made fat" (Proverbs 11:25). Removing encumbrances simplifies life and, as a bonus, others may benefit.

2. PLAN DAILY SCHEDULES IN WRITING. Do not just operate on whim. Advance planning helps avoid being bored one day and overworked another. Putting things in writing frees the mind from remembering minor necessities and allows it to focus on the more essential things. A simple step like keeping on the refrigerator a running grocery list can save a lot of frustration and needless trips to the supermarket.

3. EVALUATE DAILY ROUTINES AND READJUST WHERE HELPFUL. Every day has its more difficult moments. For many, the morning hours and the hour before supper are the hardest. During rough spots see if any activities can be changed to a less pressured time of the day. For example, if the morning hour is rushed and frantic because school lunches have to be made, learn to make the lunches the night before and leave them in the refrigerator for your husband or children to grab the next morning. Some women start preparations for supper in the morning.

4. ELIMINATE WASTED MOTIONS. Putting something away later takes twice as much work. The false convenience of temporarily setting it down is an open gate to clutter and confusion. Learn to increase the value of actions where possible. Making a double batch of spaghetti is as simple as preparing an amount for one meal. The sauce can be frozen for a fast meal on another day. I sometimes iron or fold clothes while I give my boys a spelling test. Buy a long cord for your telephone so you can extend it to a work area and fold socks or wash dishes while you talk.

Recognize that some things do not need to be done. Do not be cowed into unnecessary housework. A house should be reasonably clean, but the windows do not need to be washed every day. It is not necessary for floors to always be clean enough to eat off of like a plate. People are not supposed to eat off the floor. I know a home where the homemaker keeps everything in place and extremely clean. When you come to visit her she follows you from the front door with the vacuum cleaner. The chrome in her bathroom fixtures shine like new. Her stove looks unused. (Often it is. They eat most of their meals out. It's too much work for her to clean up the kitchen if she cooks.) Would you like to live in her home?

Developing Expertise in Budgeting

Waiting and planning are two key concepts in budgeting.

1. DO NOT PRESUME ON THE FUTURE. Our instant culture make self-restraint difficult. Instead or purchasing items on credit, wait until the item can be purchased with cash (Proverbs 22:7; Romans 13:8). Frequently, during the delay, the item becomes available in a more economical way. One couple gave up the opportunity to buy a new refrigerator on sale. A month later they purchased a larger one for half the price.

2. PLAN AHEAD TO AVOID NEEDLESS EXPENDITURES. Grocery shopping is a major area where pre-planning saves money. Mary Bouma demonstrates the value of

planning by reporting how "studies have shown that wives working outside the home spend up to twice as much for food as those who remain at home."[1] Shopping lists from preplanned menus prevent waste in groceries. Lack of time to thoughtfully plan menus or shop for bargains often leads to the purchase of more expensive, less nutritious "convenience" foods.

3. CHECK ATTITUDE TOWARDS MATERIAL POSSESSIONS. True happiness and lasting joy are not contingent upon financial status, but on the level of one's relationship with the Lord. "Thou hast put gladness in my heart, more than in the time that their corn and their wine increased," exclaimed David, the psalmist. "I will both lay me down in peace, and sleep; for thou, Lord, only makest me dwell in safety" (Psalm 4:7,8).

As Christians, we are stewards of the Lord's money. We are exhorted to make use of the world, but not full use (1 Corinthians 7:30-31). Eternal matters should take precedence over temporal gain (Luke 16:9-13; Matthew 6:19-34). In fact there are many perils to prosperity. Riches may cause people to forget God (Deuteronomy 8:13-14; Proverbs 30:8-9a), develop greediness (Psalm 62:10), miss eternal salvation (Matthew 19:23), live a barren, unfruitful life (Mark 4:19), and yield to various other temptations (1 Timothy 6:9).

4. LEARN TO SEPARATE NEEDS FROM WANTS. God promises to supply all our needs (Psalm 145:10-15; Philippians 4:19), but not all our wants (James 4:3; 1 John 2:16). Evaluate current desires by asking questions such as these: Will it increase my effectiveness for the Lord? Is it frivolous or legitimate? Is the object essential or with creativity can the need be met without buying something new? One family with small children, for example, desired a record player, but the budget did not permit any extra purchases. Using a cassette tape player the mother designed unique tapes for the children's enjoyment. Together they narrated stories complete with sound effects. In time they received a record player as a gift, but they also have priceless tapes in their own voices.

5. REMEMBER A DOLLAR SAVED IS MORE THAN A DOLLAR EARNED. Only a portion of each earned dollar reaches the worker. Money is deducted from paychecks for taxes, retirement, and so forth. When a woman saves a dollar from grocery spending, she saves a complete dollar. A woman who carefully spends the household funds may be able to contribute as much or more to the family income as a woman working full-time outside the home.

Improving Meal Planning

There are two main purposes for eating: survival and celebration. Both should be considered in planning family meals. We have to eat to sustain life. The quality of the food determines how well it can physically nourish. However, eating is more than a physical necessity. It can be the center of fellowship. A woman should consider both aspects of meals--necessity and aesthetic needs.

1. EVALUATE THE NUTRITIONAL VALUE OF FOODS. Nourishment should be an obvious reason for eating, but unfortunately in modern times taste or price alone is often the criteria for food selection. Grocery stores sell chemical compounds that are advertised to "taste like the real thing". The taste buds may not know the difference, but the human body is designed to be nourished by genuine food, not chemical substitutes. One mother, a college graduate, bragged that she saved a great deal each month by giving her under-nourished looking daughter artificial fruit drink in place of milk. In future years she will pay for false economy in doctor bills and suffering. Poor nutrition encourages gluttony (devitalized food is not satisfying, so one tends to overeat), hyperactivity, low blood sugar, and other emotional and physical disorders.

A woman is responsible to guard her family's health. Neva Coyle, founder of Overeaters Victorious, shared that "letter after letter arrives at the OV office from women who are discovering that they are the major cause of their family's poor eating habits." [2] Even a simple choice, like the selection of flour, can have an effect in a family's well-being and vitality. Psalm 104:15 speaks of God having created "bread which strengtheneth man's heart" or, according to the NASB's rendering, "sustains man's heart". Yet refined wheat products are totally devoid of vitamin E, a nutrient known to be essential to normal cardiovascular system. In several generations since the widespread introduction of white flour, coronary thrombosis has changed from a rare medical problem to the status of being the number one killer in the United States.[3]

2. CONSIDER THE AESTHETIC QUALITY OF MEALTIMES. More than a daily necessity of life, cooking should be approached as an art form. God has given us taste buds, a delicate sense of smell and a deep appreciation for texture and color. He has also created diversified selection of foods to help satisfy our different senses. Each meal should be planned for eye appeal and variety. Little touches can make even a simple plate of food a thing of beauty and give dignity and fulfillment to the one who prepared it. Digestion is enhanced by pleasant surroundings and tasty food.

3. CONSIDER SOCIAL NEEDS. Upsetting topics should be avoided at the dinner table. The climate at meals should include esteem, mutual interest and love. Even the best meal cannot compensate for negative spirits among those at the table. "Better a dinner of herbs where there is love than a fattened calf with hatred" (Proverbs 15:17 NKJV). "Better a dry crust with peace and quiet than a house full of feasting with strife. (Proverbs 17:1).

Utilizing Creativity in Decorating

God gives a woman an eye for detail that others appreciate even when they cannot define the source. Great expenditures are not necessary. One Valentine's Day a young student wife decided to surprise her husband by utilizing things on hand to create an atmosphere of love. With an odd piece of red checked fabric she made a tablecloth and matching napkins for their tiny round kitchen table. She cut an empty toilet paper tube into one inch sections and covered them with scraps of red velvet material to make attractive napkin rings. For a centerpiece she decorated red candles with gold hearts cut from the valentine he had sent her the year before. Surrounding the candles she placed heart shaped leaves which she picked from a plant in their yard. Background music helped complete the mood. At first she was hurt because when her husband came home he did not give immediate attention to the details. But the explanation of his delay in commenting on the table was eye-opening. "I didn't know exactly what it was", he bashfully admitted, "but I sensed something was special." Even if others do not notice all the creative touches in the home, they will appreciate the effect.

A woman should create a pleasing home environment, an atmosphere that represents each of the people living there. For example, in our home the walls are painted a brighter color than I would have personally selected. My husband had a strong preference that I chose to accomodate. Personality can be communicated through the things purchased or originally made. Any place, whether tiny or large, a hut or a palace, needs the continuity of creative expressions that spell "me". One young lady has cherished for years a hand-made quilt her grandmother gave her as a child. The blanket has traveled with her around the world, helping to make new, and sometimes temporary, residences a place where she belonged.

Conclusion

Homeworkers have been classified appropriately as home executives. Administering a smooth household includes organizing the home, appropriating funds for household expenditures, and planning attractive and nutritious meals. The woman of the house functions as a nurse, a gardener, a cleaning engineer, an interior designer, a child-care expert, a laundress, and a lady-of-all-trades.

A woman's job is more than changing diapers and mopping floors, although these things need to be done. A woman sets the emotional tone of life. Home should be a place of renewal and rest, a refuge from the conflicts of the outside. By absorbing the hurts others feel in the world, a woman can offer stability, beauty and love.

---

1 Bouma, Mary. The Creative Homemaker. (Bethany Fellowship: Minneapolis, Minnesota), 1973. pp. 100-101. Used by permission.

2 Chapian, Marie. Free To Be Thin. (Bethany House Publishers: Minneapolis, Minnesota), 1979. p. 53. Used by permission.

3 Nichols, Joe D., M.D. "Please Doctor, Do Something!" (Devin-Adair Co.: Old Greenwich Connecticut), 1976. p. 12. Used by permission.

DORCAS: A WOMAN WHO DID GOOD

1. Read Acts 9:36-42. What group of people wept after Dorcas died? Do you think Dorcas helped do good to others for her own selfish reasons? Why or why not?

2. Describe the Lord's attitude towards afflicted people.

    Deuteronomy 10:17-19

    Psalm 10:14

    Psalm 68:5

    Psalm 146:9

3. When we minister to the needy, whom do we help, according to Matthew 25:34-45?

4. What promise does God give to the people who care for those who cannot repay the kindness (Deuteronomy 14:29; Isaiah 58:10-11)?

5. Can you think of things to avoid in reaching out to those in affliction?

    What are some ways you can help an afflicted person you know?

    Give some guidelines for writing a good letter of comfort.

6. Is there someone you can comfort this week through a letter or an act of kindness?

DORCAS: A WOMAN WHO DID GOOD

"She stretcheth out her hand to the poor;
yea, she reacheth forth her hands to the needy"
(Proverbs 31:20).

Healthy, strong fishermen can die young in treacherous weather. Seaport towns often have a larger than average portion of widows. A place of hurt can be a place of opportunity. "Now in Joppa there was a certain disciple named Tabitha (which translated in Greek is called Dorcas): this woman was abounding with deeds of kindness and charity, which she continually did" (Acts 9:36, NASB).

Dorcas, like the Proverbs 31 woman, reached out to the poor (those in need physically), and the needy (those hurting emotionally or spiritually). We do not know Dorcas's age or marital status, but she received honor as the only woman in Scripture called a disciple, which can be defined as a learner and doer, a devoted follower of Jesus. She lived for others. Dorcas, sensitive to suffering in her coastal village, reached out to those in distress. She extended deeds of kindness <u>not</u> just occasionally, but continually.

What Are Poorly Chosen Words a Woman Like Dorcas Might Avoid?

Maybe Dorcas herself had been widowed. At any rate, she seemed to understand the true needs of those in crisis. She had discernment and the wisdom to know that some attempts to console only magnify the problem. In trying to learn more about ministering to people in distress, I reviewed the way people responded to me when my baby and later my first husband died. I also interviewed others I knew who had experienced serious trials. I asked them what attempts to comfort failed and why. There were four common expressions that seemed to frustrate rather than comfort:

1. "I KNOW JUST HOW YOU FEEL." No one knows how the other person feels. There may have been similar experiences, but no two people are alike. Telling some people you know how they feel agitates them rather than comforts. Only God knows exactly how your friend feels. Recognize your inadequacy to fully identify, but point your friend to the One who does know exactly how she feels. Remind her that He cares.

2. "I KNOW YOU MUST HAVE ASKED 'WHY?' MANY TIMES". Everyone going through an anguishing period does not ask, "Why?" Few people have suffered as intensely as Job and yet in responding to devastating trials he did not doubt God's goodness. "Job arose, and rent his mantle, and shaved his head, and fell down upon the ground, and <u>worshipped</u>. And said, 'naked came I out of my mother's womb, and naked shall I return thither: the LORD gave, and the LORD hath taken away; blessed be the name of the LORD. In all this Job sinned not, nor charged God foolishly" (Job 1:20-22). NKJV says "nor charge God with wrong." NASB says, "nor did he blame God."

3.   YOU ARE SO STRONG. I COULD NEVER ENDURE WHAT YOU'VE GONE THROUGH." The person undergoing trial did not choose the conflict. It is an encouragement when the afflicted know that others recognize the special strength which the Lord has provided; but, it is an unfair pressure when they think you expect them to have the source of strength in themselves. Affliction has the healthy effect of humbling a person. Trial manifests human weakness and draws one to depend on God. When pressured to be strong in herself, many women find it difficult to release their emotions in needed tears.

4. "IF YOUR HUSBAND (OR CHILD) HAD LIVED HE MAY HAVE BEEN BRAIN   DAMAGED." Statements of conjecture provide little comfort. A mother losing a child is not relieved to hear how the child may have been retarded if it had lived. Such thoughts focus on the trial. Such attempts to comfort are shallow and empty. A wise comforter gives encouragement based on truth, not sentimentality.

<u>How Can We Become an Effective Comforter Like Dorcas?</u>

We've all heard stories of weak attempts to comfort. Sometimes in fear of saying or doing the wrong thing, we pull away and say nothing. Dorcas is remembered for her acts of kindness and love. How can we develop sensitivity and compassion?

1. SEEK THE SPIRIT'S WISDOM. Each person has unique needs. Words deeply meaningful to a mature Christian might appear preachy to a less committed individual. An unsaved person can be challenged to look to the Lord, but it would be erroneous to encourage her to claim promises given conditionally to believers. The most useful purpose of her trial would be realizing her need to get right with God.

The Lord knows the heart and need of the person suffering. Pray for His leading. "The Lord God has given Me the tongue of the learned, that I should know how to speak a word in season to him who is weary. He awakens Me morning by morning, He awakens My ear to hear as the learned." (Isaiah 50:4, NKJV).

2. COMMUNICATE LOVE AND CONCERN.   Identify with the grief. "Rejoice with them that do rejoice and weep with them that weep" (Romans 12:15). Recognize the difficulty and share in the fellowship of the suffering, but do not pity. Some people erroneously equate comfort with placating or sympathizing. But the word comfort comes from the root word *fortis* meaning strong. Pity weakens one in trial. The sufferer does not need to be consoled; she needs to be undergirded with concern and strength. Instead of diminishing the problem, a godly comforter will recognize the hurt but build up the resources (Hebrews 12:11-12).

3. USE THE BIBLE TO ENCOURAGE. We are inadequate to comfort another person in our own power, but a well chosen verse of Scripture can strengthen and revive. "My soul," cried the Psalmist, "is weary with sorrow; strengthen me according to your word... My comfort in my suffering is this: Your promise preserves my life" (Psalm 119:28,50).

One set of verses that helped me during my husband's terminal illness was Isaiah 43:1-4. God had faithfully carried me through the waters and the rivers and, as death drew near, He took me through the fire. I was especially touched by verse 4. The One who redeemed me promised, "You are precious and honored in my sight and. . . I love you."

4. CONCENTRATE ON THE CHARACTER OF GOD. "Our Lord Jesus Christ himself, and God, even our Father, which hath loved us, and hath given us everlasting consolation and good hope through grace, comfort your hearts, and stablish you in every good word and work" (2 Thessalonians 2:16-17). Reassure the afflicted by focusing on attributes like His faithfulness, justice, all powerfulness and lovingkindness.

5. SHARE WAYS GOD HAS COMFORTED YOU. "Blessed be God, even the Father of our Lord Jesus Christ, the Father of mercies, and the God of all comfort; who comforteth us in all our tribulation, that we may be able to comfort them which are in any trouble, by the comfort wherewith we ourselves are comforted of God." (2 Corinthians 1:3-4).

One of the most uplifting passages to my husband and me during Steve's last days was a Psalm a Christian said had been especially meaningful to her mother who died of cancer two years earlier (Psalm 63).

6. EMPHASIZE AN ETERNAL PERSPECTIVE. "For our light affliction, which is but for a moment, worketh for us a far more exceeding and eternal weight of glory; while we look not at the things which are seen, but at the things which are not seen: for the things which are seen are temporal; but the things which are not seen are eternal" (2 Corinthians 4:17-18). After my husband's death, I found comfort when a friend shared Psalm 146. The God who reigns forever sustains the widow and orphans.

7. PRAY SPECIFICALLY. "In the day when I cried thou answered me and strengthenest me with strength in my soul" (Psalm 138:3). Prayer heals. Pray for and with the one struggling. Make specific requests. Ask for deliverance from any bitterness, for a meeting of practical needs. Without my knowing, while I prayed that I would be content as a single parent, many prayed for a husband for me. God answered both prayers.

How Can we Write Effective Letters of Comfort?

A valuable but often overlooked method of comforting, which Dorcas may or may not have used, is the written note. **Even though the letter of comfort is one of the best methods of supporting a friend undergoing trial, many people unnecessarily hesitate to write.** Perhaps they fear saying the wrong thing might intensify suffering. Job's companions compounded his misery. Their tactless, inaccurate verbal assault has earned for them the sarcastic name of "Job's comforters".

However, fear of making hurtful blunders should not immobilize us. Ignoring the suffering person is unkind. **Rally reinforcements and supportive strength, but do not pull away from a friend, making her feel alone and deserted.** Forsaking the downcast is a poor way to avoid saying the wrong words.

Well-written letters are a non-threatening link to the outside world. Like a soothing balm, a well written condolence letter uplifts without demanding instant feedback. A correspondent never overstays a visit, tiring the troubled. The grieving person feels no obligation to entertain the letter writer. A grieving person may reread a letter many times while a visit is only once.

How Can We Support Good Wishes with Actions?

Individuals in crisis need comforting words, but they also depend on load-lifting support. Dorcas abounded in loving deeds. She worked to meet legitimate needs. If a woman lacked clothing, she bought cloth and sewed garments for her. She provided ministry in tangible ways.

James warned, "If a brother or sister is naked and destitute of daily food, and one of you says to them, 'Depart in peace, be warmed and filled,' but you do not give them the things which are needed for the body, what does it profit? (James 2:15-16).

In contrast the prophet Isaiah promised:

> And if you spend yourselves in behalf of the hungry and satisfy the needs of the oppressed, then your light will rise in the darkness, and your night will become like the noonday. The Lord will guide you always; he will satisfy your needs in a sun-scorched land and will strengthen your frame. You will be like a well-watered garden, like a spring whose waters never fail (Isaiah 58:10-11).

The Mediterranean Sea area has one of the best climates in the world—moderate year round. But how much more refreshing to bask in the spiritual climate created by a Dorcas, a servant of the Lord. Such workers are few and when they are gone they are deeply missed. Her friends wept at her death. Her passing left a void not easily filled (Acts 9:36-42).

Would your death make a difference to those around you in need? God expresses repeatedly his special concern for the widows and orphans. He is touched by their tears. The Lord honored Dorcas for her life of service by supernaturally raising her back to life (Acts 9:40-42).

How can someone be helpful like Dorcas today? What are ways of encouraging afflicted people? Needs will vary but common ways to help include cleaning (laundry, household, dishes), cooking, mending, running errands, weeding a garden, offering transportation, caring for the sick, shopping, organizing outings, baby-sitting, and giving creative gifts of time or money. A special cassette tape can pick up the day for a sick person. Work within the realm of your natural gifts, which may not necessarily be cooking or sewing. My spiritual gift is teaching. I let single parents attend my <u>Teaching Reading at Home</u> training classes tuition free.

Tailor the gifts to the individual. A health-conscience person may prefer a bowl of fruit to a box of candy. As a new widow, after caring for my dying husband for months, I appreciated some special attention. Before the memorial service one friend took me shopping for new clothes and another friend gave me a facial and a hair cut. Thoughtful deeds ease hurt and speed up recovery for the afflicted.

Conclusion

God wants to see women like Dorcas who learn how to be true comforters—ones who do not compound a trial, but in an understanding way, help reinforce the afflicted and lift them above the trial. Hurting people need women who do not express awkwardness or discomfort, the attitude that makes the bereaved feel like they have the plague. They desire women who can greet their friends with an uplifting statement like, "I'm sure you're feeling the power of the prayers of the Christians," a comment that does not deny the depth of the crisis, but lifts the focus to a higher power. They long for women who realize that pity is unhealthy because when we start looking down, like Peter when he walked on water, we will start sinking fast (Matthew 14). When we look up we can walk above the waves of trials in victory.

A Dorcas can be counted on to help practically. She delights in serving those who cannot return the favor (James 1:27). Her labor is for the Lord.

ENCOURAGING GOOD DEEDS

1. The Titus 2 woman is to be good and to teach others to do good. What are some ways a woman can do good?

   List the forms of doing good named in 1 Timothy 5:10.

2. Consider what is involved in bringing up children spiritually. How might Timothy's upbringing encourage one living in a home that lacks male spiritual leadership (2 Timothy 1:5; 3:14-17)?

3. Name at least two reasons for showing hospitality to strangers (Hebrews 13:2; Deuteronomy 31:12).

   Describe a time when you entertained a stranger or when you were the stranger welcomed by others. What was the result?

   What other kinds of people should we open our homes to?

   What should be our motive (Luke 6:35; 14:12-14)?

4. Why do verses like Galatians 6:10 emphasize serving fellow Christians? Can you think of an example when an unbeliever was touched by observing the love Christians showed to each other?

   Phoebe served many, including the Apostle Paul (Romans 16:1-2). What are some ways she might have served?

5. One vital form of doing good is sharing the good news with unsaved people. Name one person you would like to witness to this week. Pray for an opportunity.

6. Another vital ministry to others is prayer. Share a recent answer to intercessory prayer (prayer for another person).

   List some other practical ministry opportunities available in your local church.

ENCOURAGING GOOD DEEDS

"Teachers of good things... that they may teach the young women...
to do good... that the word of God be not blasphemed"
(Titus 2:3,5).

A house full of relatives sat around Nanny's dining room table waiting for another of her delicious home-cooked meals. As she started the platter of fried chicken she reminded her family, as she had many times before, to save the back of the chicken for her. The relatives greedily searched through the plate for the best pieces, repeating to each other, "Don't forget to save the back for Nanny".

Not until years later did the granddaughter realize that the back of the chicken is mostly bone. Nanny, a poor widow, claimed it as her favorite because she delighted in serving others, unobtrusively giving them the best.

The child, the daughter of unsaved parents, was ten years old when Nanny died. But the impact of her godly testimony lingered. She remembered Nanny singing in the kitchen, reading her Bible beside the old wood cook stove, or kneeling by her bed in prayer. Thirteen years after Nanny's death the granddaughter committed herself to the Lord. Although for a while she had no living Christian woman to model her life after, the memory of Nanny's life of faith gave her direction and inspiration.

Tapping a Woman's Influence for Good

Women have a tremendous power for good or evil. The Scriptures note some women for their negative influence. Eve prompted the downfall of the most innocent man who ever lived (Genesis 3:6). Delilah was responsible for the humiliation of the strongest man who ever lived (Judges 16:16-21). Solomon's wives were credited for spiritually hardening the wisest man who ever lived (1 Kings 11:3-4).

But just as some women lead individuals astray, others are responsible for a positive impact on people. Lydia led her household to the Lord (Acts 16:14-15). Because of Rahab's faith all her kindred were saved from the destruction of Jericho (Joshua 6:25). Countless women by the living example of a meek and quiet spirit have led their husbands into a proper relationship with God (1 Peter 3:1-2). Just as a wicked woman will have a negative influence on three to four generations (Exodus 34:7b), the godly woman passes on blessing to her offspring for consecutive generations. "The mercy of the LORD is from everlasting to everlasting upon them that fear him and his righteousness unto children's children" (Psalm 103:17).

There are a number of ways a woman can positively influence her community as

---

well as her home. Some key areas of a woman's potential outreach are summarized in 1 Timothy 5:10: "well reported for good works, if she has brought up children, if she had lodged strangers, if she has washed the saints' feet, if she has relieved the afflicted, if she has diligently followed every good work." NASB says "if she has shown hospitality to strangers."

Bringing Up Children

Some women blame their husbands for the problems of their children. Although it is true that the father is the spiritual head of the home, the mother is also a dynamic influence. Even if the father is not properly leading the family, the woman has a major responsibility in positively nurturing the little ones. Without undermining his authority, she can teach the children about the Savior.

Eunice and Lois are encouraging examples from the Scriptures of a mother and grandmother who successfully instructed the child Timothy. The father was an unbelieving Greek (Acts 16:1-3), but Eunice and Lois had a sincere faith (2 Timothy 1:5) which Timothy claimed for himself. From childhood he learned the Scriptures. He recognized early that the Bible is inspired by God and valuable to equip a man for every good work (2 Timothy 3:14-17). Eunice and Lois imparted not just theoretical knowledge. They modeled before him a life of faith. Following their example, he became a dedicated disciple and one of Paul's most trusted co-laborers. Timothy gained a maturity while he was young (1 Timothy 4:12) that made it possible for him to have many fruitful years of ministry.

Lodging Strangers

Hospitality to strangers is commended often in Scripture. "Do not neglect to show hospitality to strangers, for by doing so some have entertained angels without knowing it" (Hebrews 13:2, NASB). Surprising blessings may be in store for ministering to strangers. The Israelites were challenged to be gracious to foreigners "for ye know the heart of a stranger", they were told, "seeing ye were strangers in the land of Egypt" (Exodus 23:9).

A key opportunity for believers is to open their home to international students, immigrants, or refugees. "Gather the people together, men and women, and children, and the stranger that is within thy gates, that they may hear, and that they may learn, and fear the Lord your God and observe to do all the words of this law: and that their children which have not known any thing, may hear, and learn to fear the Lord your God" (Deuteronomy 31:12-13). Converted foreigners can return to their homelands as effective missionaries (2 Chronicles 6:32-33).

<u>Ministering to Christians</u>

Phoebe stands as a scriptural example of a woman who ministered to many saints. We can only imagine ways she might have helped. The Bible names only one specific way she served. She was believed to have been entrusted as the messenger to deliver Paul's correspondence from Cenchrea, the eastern port of Corinth, to the church at Rome. The long, dangerous journey over land and sea was a challenging mission for a woman. Paul had postponed his visit to Rome many times, and it would be three more years before he could go there personally. But he trusted Phoebe to carry the letter that would one day become the New Testament book of Romans. Paul asks that she be received well and commends her for her past service to many, including himself (Romans 16:1-2).

1. HELPING LEADERS. Phoebe served as a load-lifter for Paul. He personally benefited from her ministry. She may have used domestic skill or she may have provided back-up support in the ministry. Her faithful prayer support strengthened him and her cheerful cooperative spirit undergirded him. Believers have a special responsibility to meet the needs of spiritual leaders. "Let the elders that rule well be counted worthy of double honor, especially they who labor in the word and doctrine" (1 Timothy 5:17).

2. SERVING BELIEVERS. Phoebe helped many. She used her spiritual gifts for the benefit of the body, perhaps by exhorting, counseling and encouraging. A practical servant, Phoebe gave of her talents and energies to demonstrate love to her fellow believers.

<u>Relieving the Afflicted</u>

The afflicted are dependent on others. We need to serve them without expecting recompense. Sometimes individuals face crisis situations that require temporary assistance. Examples of short-term affliction include such things as illness, the birth of a child, or a death in the family. Practical assistance during such times of need might include taking over meals, cleaning house, running errands, baby-sitting the children, doing laundry and so forth.

Other forms of affliction are long-term trials. The Lord frequently encourages demonstrations of love to the poor and handicapped (Luke 14:12-14) and to the widows and orphans (Deuteronomy 14:29; James 1:27).

Christopher de Vinck in his book, <u>The Power of the Powerless,</u> reveals some of the hidden benefits of outreach to the weak. He tells the story of his brother, who was born handicapped and lived for thirty-three years. De Vinck explains:

Oliver still remains the most hopeless human being I ever met, the weakest human being I ever met, and yet he was one of the most powerful human beings I ever met.

As a teacher, I spend many hours preparing my lessons, hoping that I can influence my students in small, significant ways. Thousands of books are printed each year with the hope that the authors can move people to action. We all labor at the task of raising our children, teaching them values, hoping something "gets through" to them after all our efforts.

Oliver could do absolutely nothing except breathe, sleep, eat and yet he was responsible for action, love courage, insight.

For me to have been brought up in a house where a tragedy was turned into a joy, explains to a great degree why I am the type of husband, father, writer and teacher I have become. [1]

Witnessing to the Lost

The woman at the well bubbled with enthusiasm after she received Jesus personally. As a result of her testimony many Samaritans trusted Christ. We too can actively share the Lord either at home or on the go. We can talk of Jesus or leave behind tracts at the grocery store or at the post office. We can share the gospel with the children's teachers, or the neighbor next door. The wise woman is alert to opportunities to share the good news (Proverbs 11:30).

Some of the richest chances to share may be at moments of personal trial. One couple shared their testimony with the policewoman who came out to investigate their child's crib death. When the officer arrived on the scene she overheard the couple playing their guitar and singing, "But as for me, I shall sing of Thy strength, yes, I shall joyfully sing of Thy lovingkindness in the morning, For thou hast been my stronghold, and a refuge in the day of my distress" (Psalm 59:16, NASB). This policewoman had herself lost a child by crib death and she recognized a supernatural power in their life. Three weeks later she claimed this power as her own when she prayed to receive Christ.

Praying for Others

Prayer is one of the most powerful means of doing good. Let us consider one case in point. In 1943 the Lord burdened a middle-aged lady with two prayer requests for a notoriously wicked high school in her community. She prayed that in that school (1) students would be saved and (2) that some of those students would be witnesses for Christ to the uttermost part of the earth. For eighteen years she claimed those two requests, believing that God would one day answer them in a mighty way.

In the meantime she developed a burden for a young fellow enrolled in that school. She sent him a gospel of John and faithfully prayed. Three years later God converted this sinful youth into a follower of Jesus Christ.

The boy's name was George Verwer. Before long large numbers of students in that school accepted Christ. The first part of that prayer was answered. The second part of the prayer is still being answered as the impact of Operation Mobilization (a missionary endeavor founded by George Verwer) is being felt all over the world.

There are special promises given when two or more make a request in the Lord's name. When women cannot easily gather together in person, prayer by telephone can be an effective means of praying. Young mothers in our church pray together by phone while their small children take afternoon naps. The children are not thrown off schedule and the mothers have fellowship without leaving home.

Serving in the Local Church

Many hours of support work are needed to maintain a smoothly running church. Kitchen help, general maintenance and children's work are basic need areas. Clerical help or artistic support can also be utilized for the benefit of all. Women qualified to counsel women or train other believers are always in demand as are spiritually mature camp counselors. Older women who train and exort younger women are essential.

Church fellowship meals for special events can be planned by the women. This may include not only the food preparation, but also ways to incorporate teaching with the activity. For example, we make place cards with Bible verses fitting for the occasion. On Resurrection Sunday we hide stuffed lambs for the children to find in a hunt. We explain that the world celebrates the day with silly, meaningless symbols like rabbits and eggs. Rabbits don't lay eggs. We ask, "Why would lambs be more appropriate?" (Jesus was the Lamb of God that was slain.)

The possibilities for service are numerous and varied. Everyone is needed. God's priceless woman is constantly searching for opportunities to minister to the believers and do good to the unsaved. Her ministry begins at home and then reaches out to individuals and corporate needs. She is used by God to positively change the lives of countless others.

"And let us not be weary in well doing: for in due season we shall reap, if we faint not. As we have therefore opportunity, let us do good unto all men, especially unto them who are of the household of faith" --Galatians 6:9-10

---

1 DeVinck, Christopher, "The Power of the Powerless", as quoted in <u>The Christian Reader</u>, July/August, 1988, p. 103.

REBEKAH: A WOMAN WHO BETRAYED HER HUSBAND

1. Read Genesis 27:1-35, 41-46. What do you see lacking in Isaac and Rebekah's relationship (Genesis 25:23;27:5-17)?

2. What effect did her lack of submission have on others?

   her husband (27:33)

   Jacob (27:19-20, 43)

   Esau (27:41; 28:8-9)

   What personal effect did Rebekah's actions have (27:43-46)?

3. Did Rebekah meet her husband's needs as described in Ephesians 5:22,33? Do you think she was an easy wife for Isaac to love? Explain.

4. Share an example from your life when you were either submissive or unsubmissive. What were the results?

5. How might a single woman model submission, thereby encouraging a married woman to submit to her husband?

6. Name one specific way this week you want to encourage your husband or God-given leader.

REBEKAH: A WOMAN WHO BETRAYED HER HUSBAND

*"The heart of her husband doth safely trust in her so that he shall have no need of spoil.
She will do him good, not evil, all the days of her life"*
(Proverbs 31:11-12).

She knew without a doubt God's will in the matter. An angel of the Lord had appeared to Rebekah. The heavenly messenger announced God's plan. Contrary to the tradition of the day, their older twin would serve the younger (Genesis 25:21-23; Romans 9:10-12). But Isaac preferred the manly firstborn, Esau (Genesis 25:27-28). Years later when Rebekah overheard Isaac prepare to bless his favored son, she hurried to thwart the plan. The Proverbs 31 woman's husband could praise his wife, but not so Isaac.

Beautiful Rebekah had great potential. She, by faith, had voluntarily left her family to travel 550 miles to a strange land and marry a man she knew God had selected for her (Genesis 24:56-61). Seeing her future mate for the first time, she covered herself with a veil (Genesis 24:64-65). This simple act perhaps foreshadowed the head coverings worn by Christian women during worship times as a symbol of submission to male leadership in the church (1 Corinthians 11:1-16). Rebekah deferred to Isaac and he responded to her with love (Genesis 24:67). It was a storybook romance, but they did not live happily ever after.

Rebekah's Response to Her Husband's Mistake

Leaders make mistakes, and Isaac was no exception. When it came time to bless his children, Isaac's personal preference overshadowed the Lord's will. He should have realized that the firstborn had questionable character for inheriting the spiritual blessing. Esau lightly esteemed that which the Lord considered holy (Genesis 25:29-34; Hebrews 12:16) and sold his birthright for a bowl of lentil soup. Much to the sorrow of his parents, he also married a heathen woman (Genesis 26:34-35).

Rebekah saw her husband blunder and she forgot to focus on her own accountability to God. She could have reminded Isaac of the angel's prophesy and left the results up to Lord. Instead she decided to take matters into her own hands. Although she had once been able to trust God, now she felt she needed to help Him out. She decided to deceive her husband and cheat Esau. She got her way because God willed for Jacob to receive the blessing, but she suffered for her sinful behavior. Her disloyal, scheming actions negatively affected the entire family, causing her unnecessary personal grief, and producing bad ramifications for future generations. Her decision to usurp the leadership from Isaac impacted her life, the lives of her immediate family, and the lives of the people in the community.

1. EFFECT OF HER LACK OF SUBMISSION ON HER FAMILY.

a. Isaac. Instead of being a helpmate Isaac could trust, Rebekah set herself at odds with her mate, causing him grief (Genesis 27:33). Things may have ended differently had Rebekah trusted the Lord to work through her husband. She could have reminded him of the angel's promise that Esau should serve Jacob. She wrongly assumed he would never listen. Yet he later responded to her appeals in another area. After she expressed her concern that Jacob not marry a Hittite woman, Isaac called his son and commanded him to seek a wife in Padden Aram from the house of his mother's father (Genesis 27:46;28:1). In fact the Lord honored Isaac's response to the children: "By faith Isaac blessed Jacob and Esau concerning things to come" (Hebrews 11:20).

b. Jacob. Her sons lost peace that could have been theirs. Jacob learned to be sneaky and dishonest. He tricked his father and lied three times to cover his deceit (Genesis 27:18-30). Later Jacob learned the hard way that a deceiver will be deceived. First, his father-in-law tricked him (Genesis 29:25), and then his own children misled him (Genesis 37:31-35). He reaped his deed of deception through twenty years of servitude to Laban and twenty-two years of sorrowing needlessly over his son Joseph. Seventeen years before his death at 147, Jacob said, "few and unpleasant have been the days of my life" (Genesis 47:9 NASB).

c. Esau. "Esau hated Jacob because of the blessing wherewith his father blessed him; and Esau said in his heart... 'I will slay my brother Jacob'" (Genesis 27:41). Because he had been deceived by his mother and brother, he developed bitterness that consumed him. He purposely decided to displease his family. When he heard they did not want Jacob to marry a Canaanite woman, out of spite he married the daughter of Ishmael (Genesis 28:8-9).

2. PERSONAL CONSEQUENCES OF REBEKAH'S LACK OF SUBMISSION.
When Rebekah overheard Esau's plan to murder Jacob, she quickly exiled the son she sought to exalt by improper means. She never again saw her favorite son. When he returned twenty years later, she was dead.

3. EFFECT OF HER LACK OF SUBMISSION ON NATIONS.
Esau's bitterness toward the brother who supplanted him passed on to succeeding generations. For centuries the Edomites, Esau's descendants, would be the enemies of the people of Israel. In Numbers 20:18-21 they refused to let the Israelites pass through their land. Hadad, a member of the royal family of Edom, became one of Solomon's greatest enemies (1 Kings 11:14-25). When Nebuchadnezzar besieged Jerusalem he was joined by the Edomites', who helped slaughter the Jews and plunder the city. Later six different prophets denounced the Edomites' cruelty to the Jews on the day of their calamity. Noted descendants of Esau include the clan of Herods: Herod the Great who tried to kill Jesus as an infant (Matthew 2:13), Herod Antipas who sent for the head of John the Baptist to be delivered on a platter (Mark 6:14,27,28) and Herod Agrippa I who executed James and imprisoned Peter (Acts 12:1-4).

Rebekah's story illustrates the principle that one wrong does not justify another sin. Isaac's spiritual blindness was not an adequate reason for Rebekah's scheming. Two wrongs make greater sin. To break the sin pattern, someone needs to be an agent for change. Poor leadership is not an excuse for deceit.

Submission Modeled by a Single Woman

Women are not exempt from submission simply because men for some reason are not effectively leading. When women take over, men are weakened further, not helped. Men need women who are wise enough to support them so they can grow. Elizabeth Elliott learned this as a single widow on the mission field. She explained:

> "I'm hesitant to accept women who teach adult Bible classes on a regular basis. It seems to me it would be much better for a man to do that. If a woman is doing it because she says no man will, I think she is out of order. Often, men will not do it simply because women will. Then they are disobedient. But if women refused to do it, men would be found who could and would.
>
> From the very first day after my husband was killed by the Aucas, I started to teach men because I was quite literally the only person who had a Bible (We didn't as yet have a translation in their language). There was no doubt in my mind that I had to teach them. I looked at it as a temporary expediency – my job was to work myself out of a job and encourage the men to take over. It was their responsibility to run the church and not mine. I coached them on a private, individual basis for their Sunday sermons, and they did the preaching. I could have preached a better sermon, but that wasn't the point. The most important thing was that they should take responsibility in the church."[1]

Elizabeth willingly encouraged men to grow in leadership over her. It was not a question of capability. She was talented, but she expanded her gift by inspiring others to grow in leadership. She could yield her control because she recognized that God held ultimate control. Her purpose was not to manipulate people, but to glorify the Lord. She set a positive example for the married women in the Indian tribe.

Conclusion

People often claim they need to usurp authority because the leader is not functioning properly. "Someone has to do it!" is the explanation given. Rebekah is an example of how this action backfires. How much better it would have been if Rebekah had appealed to her husband, reminding him of the promise from the Lord. Perhaps Jacob would have not become a deceiver and Esau would have not had bitterness toward his brother. Esau may have been more careful in the selection of his wife (Genesis 28:8-9).

We would do well to pattern after Sarah instead. "For after this manner in the old times the holy women also, who trusted in God, adorned themselves, being in subjection unto their own husbands" (1 Peter 3:5).

Rebellion comes from false confidence in self. Submission and reverence grow out of trust in the Lord. "My soul, wait thou only upon God; for my expectation is from him" (Psalm 62:5).

---

1 Johnson, Sharon. "The Biblical Woman: But What Can She Do?" <u>Moody Monthly</u>. February 1983, p. 12.

ENCOURAGING SUBMISSION TO HUSBANDS

1. Does God-given leadership mean a right to be chauvinistic, or proud? Explain God's purpose for leadership (1 Peter 5:3-6).

   What happens when women or children lead (Isaiah 3:11-13)?

   What happens when no one is in charge?

2. Leading is not easy. What kind of support would be helpful to you if you were the leader?

   Rate yourself as a follower-supporter. While the leader is responsible to God for how he leads, you are responsible for how well you handle your role. How can the application of Matthew 7:1-5 help overcome a critical spirit towards leaders?

3. If a leader is treating you harshly what is the best step of action for the follower (1 Peter 2:18-3:6)? Why is the response important?

4. If a leader appears to be making a wrong decision, a wise follower will communicate those fears in such a spirit as to still leave the final decision with the leader. How does Daniel demonstrate this principle for appealing to the leader (Daniel 1:3-15)?

5. Is there ever an appropriate time to defy an authority figure in government, in the church, in the marriage, or on the job? Explain.

   When human authority conflicts with God's authority, who is the ultimate authority (Romans 13:1-7 and Acts 4:18-20)? Explain.

6. What results, if any, can you report from your attempt last week to encourage your husband or God-given leader?

ENCOURAGING SUBMISSION TO HUSBANDS

"Encourage young women. . . being subject to their own husbands, that the word of God may not be dishonored"
(Titus 2:4-5 NASB).

How should a Christian woman respond when her husband makes a mistake? How can she admire him when he is imperfect? One modern woman models a healthy response. To alleviate financial pressures her husband considered a risky investment. When he asked his wife's opinion she confessed, "I don't feel good about the idea. Doesn't the Bible warn against get-rich-quick schemes?"

They discussed the pros and cons, then she left the final decision with him. In her silent prayers that night she told the Lord, "I believe this investment is a mistake. If he does it we may not have money to buy groceries. But my job is not to tell him what to do. That's your responsibility, Lord. By faith I am going to trust you to care for me and see that I have something to eat."

After she prayed, she felt calm. The following weeks she watched her husband plan his purchase. He spoke of his cleverness and the money he would make. In earlier days she might have nagged him, but she had already learned that nagging only made him worse. When tempted to criticize, she would pray. God helped her remain detached and objective, like a bystander. She focused her attention on positive things. As a couple they laughed together and built happy memories.

Six months later the money scheme fell through. Instead of earning extra, the husband lost their savings. He returned home surprised, discouraged, and puzzled. As he paced the floor trying to figure what went wrong, she resisted saying, "I told you so." After some time he came to her and apologized for poorly managing their finances. Together they prayed for the needed grocery money.

He learned a lesson he never forgot because his wife stood back and gave him room to make a mistake. Their relationship together deepened and he became a stronger leader. She learned to depend on God and in a surprising way the Lord provided the needed food.

Options in Marriage

There are three options regarding leadership in marital relationships, two being unpleasant. A woman can assume responsibility for a weak man or struggle in a conflict of wills with a strong man. Or more desirably, she can find satisfaction and contentment in creatively adapting to her mate and encouraging his leadership. When a husband is weak, he feels inadequate and his wife often disdains his lack of manliness, perhaps not realizing that she is much to blame for his failure to lead. When a husband, on the other hand, has to fight for the leadership in the home, life is filled with dissension and strife. Only through God's pattern can both partners reach their fullest potential. One of the greatest ways a woman can love her husband is to submit to his leadership under God and respect his position as head of the house (Ephesians 5:22,33).

When a woman obeys and honors her husband, she, by example, trains her children how to obey and honor their parents. When a good relationship exists between mates, the woman is more inspired to live a pure life, creatively care for the home and joyfully do good. Since all people are under some God-given authority, even the single woman can model a proper attitude in supporting leaders.

Submission Defined

Submission means yielding humble and intelligent obedience to God or to God's appointed authority. It is an inner heart attitude that carries a special promise of blessing. "Humble yourselves, therefore, under the mighty hand of God, that He may exalt you in due time" (1 Peter 5:6). Submission to human leaders implies trusting God to work through them, therefore deferring to their judgments or decisions. It is spoken of as "adapting to" or "fitting in with." It can be summarized by the term "no resistance." To help clarify what submission is, we will consider what submission is not.

1. SUBMISSION DOES NOT MEAN BEING INFERIOR. Christ is equal to God the Father, yet He gave us the example of submission (Philippians 2:1-11). As Jesus in His earthly life was equal to the Father in Deity (John 10:30) and yet was subordinate to Him in authority (John 14:28), so women, though equal to men in the kingdom of God (Galatians 3:28), are subordinate to man's authority in the home and in the church (Ephesians 5:22-24; 1 Corinthians 11:3). There is no thought in the scheme of divine order of the superiority of man and the inferiority of woman either in worth or in ability. God has no desire to exalt any ego (1 Peter 5:3). The subordination of women to men is purely functional, not intrinsic.

2. SUBMISSION DOES NOT MEAN BEING STAGNANT INTELLECTUALLY. The subordinate role provides a good environment for creativity and individuality to be expressed in a wholesome way. It is God's way of drawing upon gifts of intelligence, insight, and judgment without undue pressure and responsibility. Although she is not accountable as a leader, a woman is accountable for support and help. She cannot excuse wrong actions under the guise of submission. A man is much influenced by his wife.

3. SUBMISSION DOES NOT MEAN BEING UNFULFILLED. Submission helps channel talents and abilities to greater effectiveness and thus provides true fulfillment. In following God's pattern, we are able to find our deepest satisfaction in life. When we are subject to Christ, we are liberated (2 Corinthians 3:17-18; James 1:25). When we have recognized our "team captain," we are freed from the perpetual question of "Who decides this time?"

4. SUBMISSION DOES NOT MEAN BEING WEAK. Submission is a heart attitude, not a personality attribute. In fact a "mousy" person may have a suppressed rebellion that could surprisingly erupt. A more open person will be less likely to bottle things inside. A quiet, clinging-vine wife can sabotage a man's leadership by pulling a poor-little-me routine. Without the husband realizing it, she can get her way much like a pouting child.

5. SUBMISSION DOES NOT MEAN BEING PASSIVE. It takes active, concentrated effort to help another succeed. By nature people are selfish and self-willed. Godly submission is impossible without divine help. The first sin in the universe was Satan's rebellion against God's lordship. He said in his heart, "I will ascend to heaven; I will raise my throne above the stars of God, and I will sit on the mount of assembly... I will ascend above the heights of the clouds; I will make myself like the Most High" (Isaiah 14:13-14 NASB). The temptation the serpent offered Eve was, "You will be like God" (Genesis 3:5 NASB). We have inherited this same spirit of rebellion and self-exaltation. Only through the new nature received through trusting Christ can we yield our wills to the One in authority over us.

6. SUBMISSION DOES NOT MEAN BEING A "YES-MAN." A good follower knows when to objectively point out areas of potential danger regarding decision. She does not just grit her teeth and watch her leader blunder. With a meek and quiet spirit she shares her insights, leaving the final decision to him . Two are better than one in constructive planning as long as they are not fighting for the final say. The submissive woman is a non-threatening, valuable contributor.

God Is the Ultimate Authority

We are to obey earthly authority only so far as it is in harmony with God's authority. God did not give power to earthly leaders so they could veto His own authority. As an example, the early apostles were once ordered "not to speak at all nor teach in the name of Jesus." Peter and John boldly responded, "Whether it be right in the sight of God to hearken unto you more than unto God, judge ye" (Acts 4:18-19). On the rare occasion when a human authority demands disobedience to the higher laws of God, the believer should stand for the higher authority.

What if a woman's husband or leader insists that she do something she does not consider right? For example, what if he wants her to work away from the home while she believes the Scriptures teach for her to be a keeper at home? The submissive person needs to find the reason behind her leader's desire and then provide a creative alternative. Is the reason financial strain? She might demonstrate how a second income does not always help as much as expected, especially when the wife works away from the home. The added expenses often absorb the imagined gain. A job working out of the home could be more profitable, and would not conflict with Scripture. A wife could appeal in terms the man would understand. Discuss the temptations of working away from home. In our day many women get emotionally involved with men they meet on the job. Tell him you want to be loyal to him all your life. You don't want the conflict of another boss to please. Offer to stretch the money you do have more carefully. Appeal to his protective care while helping him solve his problems in a practical way.

What should a woman do over minor differences in doctrine? One woman left her husband because he did not understand church government as she did. She wanted to worship "correctly." The higher command in Scripture is the marriage bond. A wife is to be loyal even to an unbelieving mate if he chooses to remain with her. Submission to God should not be taken to extremes to justify lack of submission to human authority.

Submission is not limited to wives. Submission is a fact of life. All people are under some authority, be it church leaders (Hebrews 13:17), parents (Ephesians 6:1-4), employers (1 Peter 2:18) or governmental officials (1 Peter 2:13-14). Even the king is under God. The injunction to submit to human authority carries the reminder that the real authority behind it all is Christ. It is God who determines who is promoted even in top offices (Psalm 75:6-7). Regarding government leaders, we are commanded to "be subject unto the higher powers. For there is no power but of God: the powers that be are ordained of God" (Romans 13:1). Elders are over us in the Lord (1 Thess. 5:12). Children still living at home are to obey parents because it is well-pleasing unto the Lord (Colossians 3:20), and we are to be submissive to employers as unto Christ (Ephesians 6:5-8).

The Chain-of-Command Structure Benefits the Followers

It is easier to submit to or reverence someone in a God-appointed position when we realize that our positive response is for our own good. For one thing we will have stronger supervisors. A leader is more concerned with his assistant's needs when he no longer has to fight for his position.

By **submitting to government leaders** and the laws of the land, we "put to silence the ignorance of foolish men" (1 Peter 2:15), receive praise from the rulers (Romans 13:3), forego punishment (Romans 13:3-4) and have a good conscience (Romans 13:5).

When we **respect church elders** and submit to their leadership, we give them joy and thereby help make their leadership profitable for us (Hebrews 13:17).

If we **esteem our husbands,** they can better do their job of cherishing and nourishing their wives (Ephesians 5:28-33).

When children **obey parents**, the adults become a God-given source of guidance and security for their off-spring (Proverbs 6:20-23).

When we **honor employers** by a diligent and faithful character we will be rewarded by the Lord according to our service (Colossians 3:22-25).

The chain-of-command structure is for our protection. Harmony comes when we display deference. Confusion results when we take matters into our own hands.

Team-Orientation Produces Success

The best athletic team is not necessarily the one with the best individual players. So it is with life. Teamwork is essential for long-range success. We should never work in competition with our leaders but always in harmony with them. The person who criticizes or usurps authority from a leader is like a volleyball player who always plays the other man's spot. The game is not improved in the long run. When one is trying to do someone else's job, what happens when his own job needs to be done? He not only weakens the player he has intimidated by revealing lack of faith in his ability, but he has also left his own spot vulnerable.

The best player to do the job in a team sport is the one assigned the job. Likewise, when a woman runs her husband down or takes over headship responsibilities in her home, she will fail in the long run. She will be unable to do her best in her assigned role as wife and mother because she will have a discouraged husband and father who will be less capable of leading. The team-oriented woman realizes her dependence on the leader. They either rise or sink together.

RUTH: A SINGLE PRICELESS WOMAN

1. Read the book of Ruth for an overview and answer the following.

   What did Ruth stand to lose when she joined Naomi (Ruth 1:8-18; 2:11)?

   What did she stand to gain?

2. Describe the main priority in Ruth's life (Ruth 1:16, 2:11-12). Paraphrase Matthew 6:33 and apply the principle to Ruth.

3. How did Boaz learn about Ruth's character (Ruth 2:11-12; 3:11)?

   Why is an objective evaluation by others an important element in selecting a mate?

4. Other than the Proverbs 31 woman (v.10, KJV), Ruth is the only woman in Scripture described as a "virtuous woman" (Ruth 3:11, KJV). Using a dictionary, define "virtuous."

   List character qualities (such as loyalty) exhibited in Ruth's life. Explain.

5. How did the Lord bless Ruth as a result of her faith? How did he use her to bless others (Ruth 4:13-22)?

6. Can you think of a situation in your life where God blessed you for your faith? Explain.

RUTH: A SINGLE PRICELESS WOMAN

"Who can find a virtuous woman?
for her price is far above rubies"
(Proverbs 31:10).

The young widow struggled to find an identity without her husband. Ruth, a Moabitess, had married the son of a Hebrew family living in her country. According to custom, Ruth was expected to remain with her in-laws until she remarried. But her husband's father and brother had also died leaving Naomi, the widowed mother-in-law, destitute. She could not care for Ruth. For her own survival she decided to return to the land of her birth.

The Israelite people did not warmly receive citizens of Moab. Moses had warned them in Deuteronomy 23:3-6, "No Ammonite or Moabite or any of his descendents may enter the assembly of the Lord, even down to the tenth generation... Do not seek a treaty of friendship with them as long as you live." Ruth could not expect a warm welcome in Naomi's country.

"Naomi said to her two daughters-in-law, 'Go back, each of you, to your mother's home. May the Lord show kindness to you, as you have shown to your dead and to me. May the Lord grant that each of you will find rest in the home of another husband.'

Then she kissed them and they wept aloud and said to her, 'We will go back with you to your people.'

But Naomi said, 'Return home, my daughters. Why would you come with me? Am I going to have any more sons, who could become your husbands? Return home, my daughters: I am too old to have another husband. Even if I thought there was still hope for me— even if I had a husband tonight and then gave birth to sons—would you wait until they grew up? Would you remain unmarried for them? No, my daughters. It is more bitter for me than for you, because the Lord's hand has gone out against me!'" (Ruth 1:8-13, NIV).

Humanly speaking, Ruth's most logical response would be to return to her parent's home. Orpah, her sister-in-law, chose that route. To accompany Naomi meant accepting the role of a foreigner and an outcast in a hostile land. Remarriage would be an unlikely possibility. Naomi, herself, had not been the most pleasant company. She felt bitter about the tragic death of her husband and sons.

But Naomi had one thing to offer Ruth that made the sacrifice worthwhile. Naomi served the one true God. Ruth had personally accepted Jehovah as her Lord. She clung to her mother-in-law.

served the one true God. Her family had tried to flee God's discipline. She learned the hard way that one cannot outrun god. Broken and suffering from the folly of her sin, she makes the right move. She decides to return to the Lord's people. Repentence and humility bring blessing from God (Psalm 146:8-9).

"Look,' suggested Naomi, "your sister-in-law has gone back to her people and her gods. Return after your sister-in-law."

Ruth replied, "Entreat me not to leave you or to turn back from following after you; for wherever you go I will go, and wherever you lodge, I will lodge. Your people shall be my people, and your God, my God " (Ruth 1:15-17 NKJV).

Ruth had personally accepted Jehovah as her Lord and for this reason she clung to her mother-in-law, her link to the Savior. Romans 10:11-13 explains the Lord's response to Ruth's decision. "For the scripture saith, Whosoever believeth on him shall not be ashamed." God prepared the way for her in Bethlehem.

A Mosaic law provided for the poor in Israel (Deut. 24:19-22). The Lord ordered Jewish harvesters to leave behind some of the grain instead of picking a field clean. Needy people could follow the workers and glean, or pick up, missed fruit or grain.

When Ruth set out to glean in the fields, there were many places she could have chosen, but providentially she selected the field of Boaz, a near kinsman. Interestingly enough Boaz had a gentile mother, Rahab the converted harlot from Jericho. He knew a gentile could be strong in the faith. His heritage lessened any reservation he would have of accepting Ruth.

God provided a way whereby a marriage between Boaz and Ruth would be acceptable culturally. The Lord ordained a Hebrew custom that offset the warning of Deuteronomy 23:3-6. In 25:5-10, Moses decreed that a childless widow can appeal to the nearest relative and request marriage to raise up children in the dead man's name.

Boaz was not obligated to redeem Ruth. He was not the closest kinsman. He chose to protect her because he had watched her life. He listened to what others said. **He recognized a woman of character, and he took the initiative to win her.**

When I lead Bible studies with single teens, or women, I frequently hear complaints about studying Proverbs 31. "That passage only frustrates me," some will say. "I don't have a husband. I can't do any of those things yet." I often answer them with the story of Ruth. The Moabitess, though unmarried, modeled all the qualities illustrated in Proverbs 31.

A woman does not need to be married with children to pattern after the Proverbs 31 ideal. Some never marry; others become single again. A mother, at one age, bears children. Later she watches her children leave home. A woman's life is seasonal, constantly changing, but character qualities transcend circumstances.

Character Qualities Modeled by Ruth

The wife of a leader in the community, the Proverbs 31 woman had maids and servants. Ruth was a poor woman working in the fields, a foreigner and a widow. Yet the same qualities made both successful.

1. FAITH. Ruth trusted personally in Jehovah (Ruth 1:16), refusing to return to the gods of her people. She sacrificed lifetime ties, culture, and identity, leaving father, mother and the land of her nativity, to come to a strange people (Ruth 2:11). Faith in Jehovah overshadowed fear of poverty, loneliness and rejection as a poor widow in a foreign land (Ruth 2:12). Like the woman in Proverbs her predominate characteristic was a fear of the Lord.

2. LOYALTY. Ruth models loyalty to her mother-in-law. "Where you die, I will die, and there will I be buried. The LORD do so to me, and more also, if anything but death parts you and me" (Ruth 1:17, NKJV). Ruth chose to renounce her pagan heritage permanently. The Proverbs 31 woman demonstrated loyalty to her husband. He safely trusted her in every way, being confident that she would bring him only good and not harm (Proverbs 31:11-12).

3. INITIATIVE. Ruth did not depend on her mother-in-law for her provision. On her own she sought a field in which to glean. The Proverbs 31 woman worked willingly with her hands, (Proverbs 31:13), giving special attention to the needs of her family (v.14,15,27). Likewise, Ruth took initiative, instead of waiting for others to coerce her.

4. DILIGENCE. Ruth finished what she started. Others noticed her steadfastness. The servant of Boaz commended her diligence (Ruth 2:3,7). She persisted day after day to complete her task (Ruth 2:23). Like the Proverbs 31 woman she could be counted on to complete a job (Proverbs 31:15,17,18,27).

5. GENEROSITY. Ruth thought of the needs of others. After working hard all day gathering barley, "she carried it back to town and her mother-in-law saw how much she had gathered" (Ruth 2:18a). For lunch Boaz had offered her some roasted grain. Ruth also brought Naomi "what she had left over after she had eaten enough" (Ruth 2:18b). The Proverbs 31 woman in a similar way cared for the needs of others, even when it meant loss of sleep for herself (Proverbs 31:15). "She opens her arms to the poor and extends her hands to the needy" (Proverbs 31:20).

6. VIRTUE. Boaz said of Ruth, "for all the city of my people doth know that thou art a virtuous woman" (Ruth 3:11). Like the Proverbs 31 woman she was noted for noble character, excellence in spirit, and purity of life (Proverbs 31:10). The descriptive phrase, "virtuous woman" is only used in Scripture these two times.

God Blesses Women of Godly Character

The virtuous woman in Proverbs received great honor. Her husband, children, and community spontaneously praised her. Because she put God first, He fulfilled her need.

Likewise, Ruth exemplifies Matthew 6:33 in action. By seeking Jehovah first, she received the desire of her heart. When she chose to follow the Lord instead of the gods of Moab, she had little hope to be more than a foreigner gleaning in the fields of Bethlehem. She must have felt like the Psalmist who cried, "I had rather be a doorkeeper in the house of my God, than to dwell in the tents of wickedness" (Psalm 84:10b). Nonetheless, the godly widow was accepted into the land, respected by the community and redeemed by a prominent leader in Israel, the owner of the fields where she gleaned. Messiah would descend from their first child (Ruth 4:17; Matthew 1:5).

From the story of Ruth, we learn that the key to major decisions is to make the Lord the main priority. We should avoid moves made for material advantage alone. Naomi and Elimelech moved to Moab to protect their health. Elimelech and his two sons died. Ruth moved to Bethlehem to serve the Lord even though the move threatened her financial security. She received blessings of which she never dreamed.

If single, our choice of activities should not focus on "catching a man." Our goal should be to deepen our relationship with God. A woman who grows spiritually is worthy of a more mature man if she marries. Even if God calls her to a life set apart for Him, she is more successful and content as a single woman because of her godly attributes.

PROVERBS 31: A MARRIED PRICELESS WOMAN

1. Reread Proverbs 31: 10-31. What new insights do you have since you first read this passage at the beginning of the course?

   Do you feel more qualified to counsel a young man on evaluating a potential mate, or a young woman on how to be a priceless woman? What has helped you the most?

2. Meditate on Proverbs 31:11-12. What is meant by "he shall have no need of spoil" (KJV)?

   How might she bring her leader good and not harm?

   What is significant about the expression, "all the days of her life?"

3. The Proverbs 31 woman's husband has complete confidence in her. From your experience, what character qualities should encourage a husband (parent, Christian leader, boss, roommate, etc.) to trust you?

   Can you think of an example from your own experience of how the violation of any of these qualities created a lack of trust?

4. List character qualities (such as creativity or initiative) evident in the Proverbs 31 woman's life. What quality would you like most to see strengthened in your own life? Why?

5. Some stretch Proverbs 31 to advocate full-time, away from the home jobs for married women with children. Does Scripture promote outside careers for wives and mothers? Where?

6. Contrast Proverbs 31 and Titus 2:3-5 with the ideas about women you commonly hear in the world today.

PROVERBS 31: A MARRIED PRICELESS WOMAN

"Charm is deceitful and beauty is vain,
but a woman who fears the Lord, she shall be praised"
(Proverbs 31:30 NKJV).

The world, elevating beauty as the secret of happiness, beckons a woman to invest hours and dollars in physical allure. What a woman cannot achieve in looks she is challenged to acquire through charm or status. People forget that circumstances change. Accidents can alter a person's dexterity or physical appearance. Illness can make an agile woman clumsy and a beautiful woman homely. A millionairess today may be a pauper tomorrow.

God says, "Favor is deceitful, and beauty is vain" (Proverbs 31:30), or in other words external qualities are not lasting in value. The best of woman's efforts to hide her true, corrupt nature are futile, empty, hollow, and transitory. The stark contrast between God's perspective and man's perspective is summarized in 1 Samuel 16:7. "For the Lord seeth not as man seeth; for man looketh on the outward appearance, but the Lord looketh on the heart." Physical beauty will fade and social status can crumble, but only inner character rooted in the person of Christ will endure the storms and adjustments of this life and pave the way to life eternal. If you have not done so already, we challenge you to repent of your pride in trying to control your life, acknowledge your sinfulness before a holy God, and call out to Him for His mercy on you a sinner.

Titus 2 Qualities Displayed in the Proverbs 31 Woman

In this course we have studied the model woman described in Titus 2:3-5 and illustrated by Proverbs 31. The first six lessons focused on the godly woman's personal walk with God. Starting in lesson seven we considered how she relates to others. She speaks with kindness (Proverbs 31:26b), displays self-control (v.29), loves her mate (v.11), loves her children (v. 28), models purity (vv. 10, 25), keeps her home (v.27), practices good works (v. 20), and supports her husband's leadership (v.23).

In action we see her modeling the Christian life (Lessons 1-2), yielding to the Lord (Lessons 3-4), worshipping her Creator (Lessons 5-6), encouraging others (Lessons 7-8), restraining her appetites and desires (Lessons 9-10), training other women (Lessons 11-12), complimenting and enhancing her husband or other leaders (Lessons 13-14), nurturing and training children (Lessons 15-16), uplifting the men in her life (Lessons 17-18), serving her family (Lessons 19-20), serving her church and community (Lessons 21-22), and adapting to her mate (Lessons 23-24).

To summarize the series we will evaluate the Proverbs woman in terms of character qualities. She mastered many practical skills, but God does not predescribe the exact actions for all women in any culture. A godly woman does not have to weave cloth, grow grapes, or work tapestry. God gave each unique woman a different combination of interests, abilities and responsibilities. To fully appreciate the example of the priceless woman we need to see how her actions mirror her soul.

Consider the Proverbs 31 passage verse by verse, looking not just at activities but at the list of characteristics revealed:

Verse-by-verse Study of Character Qualities using The New King James Version:

(v.11) DISCRETION, RESPONSIBILITY, VIRTUE, TRUTHFULNESS, THRIFTI-NESS, GRATEFULNESS, JOYFULNESS, AND VIRTUE. "The heart of her husband safely trusts her, so that he will have no lack of gain."

A husband can trust a DISCREET wife, one who is careful with words and actions. He can depend on a RESPONSIBLE partner. Dinner will be prepared in time for him to make his meeting. Clean socks will be ready for him to wear in the morning. He can trust an HONEST wife, knowing her word is reliable. With a THRIFTY mate a man does not fear needlessly losing his hard earned money because of his wife's careless spending habits. He can be assured each dollar will be used wisely.

(v.12) LOYALTY, DEPENDABILITY, AND SENSITIVITY. "She does him good and not evil all the days of her life."

(v.13) INITIATIVE, CREATIVITY, RESOURCEFULNESS, JOYFULNESS. "She seeks wool, and flax, and willingly works with her hands."

(v.14) CREATIVITY, INDUSTRIOUSNESS, AND THRIFTINESS (MEALS DIS-TINCTIVE LIKE IMPORTED SPECIALITIES). "She is like the merchants' ships, she brings her food from afar." She scouted out the bargains available in her neighborhood shops and brings them home. Maybe she belongs to a co-op where she can get farm fresh eggs, or she goes to the mill to get whole-grain flour freshly ground. She might purchase honey and grain in bulk and know the best fish market in town. She works to serve appealing meals from quality foods carefully selected.

(v.15) DILIGENCE, ORDERLINESS, AND INITIATIVE (GETS UP EARLY FOR THE BENEFIT OF OTHERS; HAS A DEVOTIONAL TIME?) "She also rises while it is yet night, and provides food for her household, and a portion to her maidservants."

(v.16) THRIFTINESS, INITIATIVE, DILIGENCE, AND RESOURCEFULNESS. "She considers a field, and buys it; from her profits she plants a vineyard." No, this verse does not make her a real estate sales person. Mary Pride in The Way Home says, "Tell me how buying shoes for your family makes you a shoe salesman and I'll be able to explain to you how buying a vineyard makes this woman a real-estate dealer! She bought one field for her family's use; she didn't re-sell it, much less make a career out of buying fields here and there and tooling around on her donkey to show the properties to prospective buyers... Housewives from time immemorial have planted gardens in their back yards, or tended truck patches on a portion of the family's forty acres."[1]

(v.17) ENTHUSIASM, DILIGENCE (PHYSICALLY FIT, SPIRITUALLY EQUIPPED -- Ephesians 6:14). "She girds herself with strength, and strengthens her arms."

(v.18) CONTENTMENT, INDUSTRIOUSNESS, AND DILIGENCE. "She perceives that her merchandise is good, and her candle does not go out by night."

(v.19) RESOURCEFULNESS AND CREATIVITY. "She stretches out her hands to the distaff, and her hand holds the spindle."

(v.20) GENEROSITY AND HOSPITALITY. "She extends her hand to the poor; yes, she reaches out her hands to the needy."

(v.21) SECURITY AND RESPONSIBILITY (PROVIDES ADEQUATE CLOTHING FOR FAMILY—PHYSICALLY AND SPIRITUALLY). "She is not afraid of snow for her household; for all her household is clothed with scarlet." The word "scarlet" in the original language has a double meaning. It can mean warm clothes but it can also refer to the color red (a symbol of the blood of Christ-- Joshua 2,18,19; Hebrews 9:19-22).

(v.22) CREATIVITY AND VIRTUE. "She makes tapestry for herself; her clothing is fine linen and purple." Linen is a symbol of righteousness (Revelation 19:8) and purple is a symbol of royalty; we are daughters of the King (Psalm 45:9).

(v.23) LOYALTY AND WISDOM (FREES HUSBAND TO SERVE WITH LEADERS OF THE LAND, COMPLETES MATE, DOES NOT COMPETE WITH HIM). "Her husband is known in the gates when he sits among the elders of the land." The husband of a virtuous woman is respected in public because he is respected at home. Likewise, he has the confidence to lead in the community because he has been successful as a leader of his family. He is not drained by constant squabbles at home. With the full support of his trustworthy wife and obedient children, he feels strengthened to lead in local issues.

(v.24) CREATIVITY, RESOURCEFULNESS, THRIFTINESS AND DILIGENCE. "She makes linen garments and sells them; and supplies sashes to the merchants." As a homeworking wife, she makes products for sale to the shop keepers. (She is not a merchant herself or a factory worker.)

(v.25) JOYFULNESS, SECURITY, PURITY, AND DISCRETION. "Strength and honor are her clothing; she shall rejoice in time to come."

(v.26) WISDOM AND SENSITIVITY. "She opens her mouth with wisdom; and on her tongue is the law of kindness."

(v.27) ORDERLINESS AND DILIGENCE. "She watches over the ways of her household, and does not eat the bread of idleness." Her concern is not making a name for herself, but looking out for her family and home.

(v.30) FAITH, SECURITY AND WISDOM. "Charm is deceitful, and beauty is vain, but a woman who fears the Lord, she shall be praised."

Conclusion

As we review this course, we should not be discouraged as we realize how many areas we need to develop. God is in the process of conforming our character more to His image, but His work is not yet finished. Consider the overall goal represented by His ideal woman as a point of challenge, but also remember that diamonds are not made in a day. Years of stress coupled with the work of skilled hands are necessary to complete the refinement of a real jewel. The overall goal is not fully achieved after studying (or writing) this book. Hopefully the vision will bring about a lifetime of changes for the better.

---

1 Pride, Mary. The Way Home. (Crossway Books: Westchester, Illinois) 1985. p. 149.

Additional Products Available from:

BackHome Industries
PO Box 22495
Milwaukie, Oregon 97269
(503) 654-2300

Helping teach
Bible in application to our lives,
History from a providential view,
Economics from a free-market perspective,
Spelling from a logical, phonics basis, and
Reading from a Christian point-of-view

*"That our sons may be as plants grown up in their youth;
That our daughters may be as pillars, sculptured in palace style."*
- Psalm 144:12

Publications of **Back Home Industries, Inc.**

Providing seminars and materials for teaching Bible, Economics, Language Arts, & History

Economics

▄ A BANKER'S CONFESSION: A Christian Guide to Getting Out of Debt by Gary Sanseri

While deficits escalate, wise economic forecasters warn Americans to get out of debt now! Here is a practical book on why and how. The author gives you the Biblical, moral foundation for "owing no man anything." A study guide provides applicational questions. Teach your children the principles of debt free living **before they get into financial problems.**

Language Arts

▄ 70 BASIC PHONOGRAMS & CASSETTE TAPE by Wanda Sanseri

English is 93 to 97% phonetically accurate IF we learn the basis of our language. Most of us were taught "look-say" (the guess method) or an inadequate amount of phonics. The 70 phonograms link the basic fixed combinations of letters in English with the sounds they make. The back of each card gives the information on how to present the phonogram like a master teacher. Cards and tape are highly recommended BEFORE taking a Teaching Reading at Home training class.

▄ TEACHING READING AT HOME by Wanda Sanseri

Educators using The Writing Road to Reading need help unlocking the hidden treasures found there. Written by a home school mom who also has experience as a school teacher and private tutor. Outstanding features of the book include the sequential guide, diagnostic tests, charts, new exercises, grammar helps and MUCH MORE! Teaching Reading at Home is the workbook for workshops by the same name. Use the book independently or, for even greater benefit, sign up for a two day training class in your area.

▄ TEACHING READING at HOME TRAINING VIDEO with Wanda Sanseri and young children

This video includes reviewing and quizzing phonograms 1-52, teaching charts 1 and 3, dictating spelling words, and reading from The New England Primer.

▄ ALPHA LIST: A DICTIONARY OF SPELLING LOGIC by Wanda Sanseri

The Alpha List analyzes the 2000 most frequently used English words, divides them into syllables using TRH spelling markings, cites the spelling rules that apply, lists derivatives, indexes them to The Writing Road to Reading and gives special comments when needed.

▄ SPELLING BOOSTERS by Wanda Sanseri.

Creative, easy to use reinforcement exercises for the spelling words in The Writing Road to Reading. Includes poems, original stories, Bible quotes, and word studies.

▄ THE NEW ENGLAND PRIMER of 1777 edited & expanded by Gary and Wanda Sanseri.

Teach reading and moral excellence with a newly typeset reprint of the textbook used by our founding fathers! Includes "I can read stories" using 99 of the most frequently used words in English.

Bible

▄ GOD'S PRICELESS WOMAN by Wanda Sanseri.

This refreshing study designed for either private, one-on-one or group study, addresses the concerns of young, old, married and single women in light of God's Word. In this 182 page study guide, Wanda encourages us to return to Scriptures for our bearings. She outlines the challenges of womanhood as summarized in Titus 2: 3-5. Application questions are written to address the needs of women at various seasons of life.

▄ ADVENT FORETOLD: A December Devotional for All Ages by Gary and Wanda Sanseri.

The theme of prophecy and fulfillment regarding the advent of Messiah is explored. Professionally drawn art enhances the daily text. Probing questions and insights help make this book a potential family heirloom to read with growing interest year after year.

History--Quality Reprints

▄ THE LIFE OF JOHN CALVIN by Theodore Beza

A definitive biography written by a contemporary of Calvin, includes an appendix with the story of his godly marriage.

▄ REMARKABLE PROVIDENCES by Increase Mather

A collection of fascinating stories that evidence God's providence in the early days of American colonization.

▄ MOODY'S CHILD STORIES by Dwight L. Moody

True stories for children by the 19th century preacher.

For Current Catalogue and Updated Prices write to: Back Home Industries; PO Box 22495, Milwaukie, OR 97269.